Out of Reach

Inequalities in the Irish Housing System

tasc *at* **NEW ISLAND** publications to date

Engaging Citizens
The Report of the Democracy Commission
Edited by Clodagh Harris October 2005

Post Washington
Why America can't rule the World
by Tony Kinsella and Fintan O'Toole June 2005

For Richer, For Poorer
Strategies for a fairer Pension System
Edited by Jim Stewart May 2005

An Outburst Of Frankness
Community arts in Ireland – a reader
Edited by Sandy Fitzgerald November 2004

Selling Out?
Privatisation in Ireland
by Paul Sweeney October 2004

After The Ball
by Fintan O'Toole October 2003

tasc

A Think Tank for Action on Social change

26 Sth Frederick St, Dublin 2.
Ph: 00353 1 6169050
Email:contact@tascnet.ie
www.tascnet.ie

Out of Reach

*Inequalities in the
Irish Housing System*

P.J. Drudy and Michael Punch

Out of Reach
First published 2005
by tasc at New Island
an imprint of New Island Press
2 Brookside
Dundrum
Dublin 14

www.newisland.ie

The authors have asserted their moral rights.

ISBN 1-904301 88 6.

British Library Cataloguing in Publication Data.
A CIP catalogue record for this book is available
from the British Library.

Typeset by Ashfield Press
Cover design by Public Communications Centre

Printed in Ireland by
Betaprint Limited, Dublin

Contents

THE AUTHORS

P.J. DRUDY took his Ph.D. degree at Cambridge University where he was formerly a Fellow of St Edmund's College and a Lecturer at the Department of Land Economy. He is currently a Fellow, Associate Professor of Economics and Co-Director of the Centre for Urban and Regional Studies at Trinity College, Dublin. He has been actively involved with a range of community organisations and public bodies. Professor Drudy has published extensively on urban and regional policy and housing and is Co-Editor of the series *Dublin: Economic and Social Trends.*

MICHAEL PUNCH took his Ph.D. degree at Trinity College Dublin where he was formerly a Threshold Research Fellow at the Centre for Urban and Regional Studies. He is currently the Broad Curriculum Lecturer in Globalisation in the Departments of Geography and Sociology at Trinity. He has also worked with many community-voluntary groups on action-research projects and in an advisory capacity. He has published on economic restructuring, local development, urban planning and housing policy in a number of Irish and international journals, including *Housing Studies, Antipode, Journal of Irish Urban Studies* and the *Journal of the Statistical and Social Inquiry Society of Ireland.*

Acknowledgements

We have drawn heavily on the work of others for this book and the final text reflects discussions with and advice and criticism from friends and colleagues over many years. While we may not have always heeded their advice, we are particularly heartened that many of the concerns we express about housing and the policies we espouse are in fact shared by a wide range of respected individuals inside and outside Ireland. We are deeply indebted to them.

We are especially indebted to Paula Clancy, Director of TASC, who encouraged us to write the book and gave us enormous support at all stages. Our thanks too to Paul Sweeney, Chairperson of the TASC Economist Network for helpful advice and guidance. We are grateful to Michael Bannon, Eoin O'Sullivan, Emmet Bergin, Paul Sweeney, Aideen Hayden, Maeve Ann Wren, Jerome Connolly, Margaret Burns, Lance O'Brien, Gus Geraghty and Joelle Grospelier who made helpful comments and suggestions on some or all of the draft manuscript. They have helped a great deal and saved us from various blunders! Our thanks too to Phill McCaughey and all those involved in the book's production.

Our colleagues in the Departments of Economics, Geography and Sociology in Trinity College have always been supportive – our particular thanks to Dermot McAleese, John O'Hagan, Alan Matthews, Andrew MacLaran, Sinéad Kelly and Bob Holton.

We have learned much about housing over the years from friends inside and outside Trinity College and in particular from those actively involved in community development. These include: Gerry Fay, Betty Ashe, Dolores Wilson, Charlie Murphy, Seanie Lambe, Micheál Collins, Loretta O'Sullivan, Jim Stewart, Tony McCashin, Declan Redmond, Pauline Faughnan, Martin Collins, Yetti Redmond, Stanislaus Kennedy, Daithi Downey, Alice Leahy, Mary Higgins, Peter McVerry, Eithne Fitzgerald, Kieran Murphy, Lillian Buchanan, Simon Brooke, Chris Paris, Joe Grennell, Sean Healy, Brigid Reynolds, Rory Guinness, Fred Stephens, Donal McManus, Bernard Thompson, Colm Rapple, Michelle Norris, Eimear Ó Siochrú, Noeleen Hartigan, John Bissett, Rita Fagan, Joe Donohue, Josephine Henry, Dorothy Walker, Lena Jordan, Charlie Hammond, John Gallagher, Paul McNulty and many more.

We received considerable support from the Department of Environment, Heritage and Local Government. In particular, we express our thanks to Des Dowling, Eugene Doyle, Máire O'Mahony and Alcie O'Reilly.

Sheelagh, Aisling, Conor, David, Aoife, Kathleen and Ethna Drudy, as always, gave their whole-hearted support, as did Marie and Eddie Punch.

Any remaining inadequacies are obviously our responsibility.

PJD
MP

Trinity College, Dublin
November 2005

Chapter 1

Irish Housing: A System of Winners and Losers?

A CELTIC TIGER CRISIS?

I f a secure, affordable, and suitable home is one of the most basic human requirements, how is it possible that Ireland – once among the poorest nations in the European Union and now one of its richest – currently has a severe housing crisis? House prices and private rents have risen beyond the reach of many, while the state provides far too few houses for those who can neither buy nor rent. Despite impressive economic gains, especially in the last decade, a substantial minority of our population are no nearer to owning a home, or renting one at a reasonable price, than they were ten years ago. Indeed the situation has likely worsened over recent years of strong economic growth, if we are to judge by unaffordable house prices, prohibitively priced and insecure private rental accommodation, a short-age of public housing, expanded waiting lists and a growing homeless population.

At the same time, Ireland holds one of the highest rates of home ownership in Europe. Many Irish also own second homes in Ireland and farther afield, while others view hous-ing as yet another market-place opportunity for investment, speculation and capital gain. Take, for example, the single detached Dublin home, requiring extensive refurbishment on 1.8 acres that sold in 2005 for a reported €58 million. Obviously what fetched this outlandish sum was mainly the land itself, ripe for re-development as either apartments or houses. A nearby house on less than one acre is currently for sale at an asking price of €30 million. The owners of similar houses frequently have one or more homes abroad, in which they claim residence – thereby enabling them to pay little or no tax here in Ireland. Whether our millionaire owners regard such houses as homes, trophies or investments, they know nothing of the difficulties that confront young first-time buyers, struggling to pay mortgages, not to mention the plight of those on low incomes who will never own a home.

In short, together with our much-hyped Celtic Tiger economy, Ireland can also boast of a housing system that is distinguished by deep inequalities and a clear-cut division between winners and losers: those who have profited hugely from our housing-for-profit boom, and those who are struggling to find or sustain a suitable roof over their heads.

While not exhaustive, Table 1.1 clearly illustrates the stark divide between those who gain from our housing system and those who do not. Winners include not just speculators who invariably gain, but also lending agencies, estate agents, solicitors, and national and provincial newspapers whose Property Supplements profit from the massive advertising campaign that accompanies a property boom. Major losers include many thousands who can never aspire to own a home and an array of social groups disadvantaged by our market-dominated system, including the unemployed, the homeless, those on low incomes, ethnic minorities, people with disabilities, tenants in private rental accommodation and thousands more who are either on the public housing lists or live in poorly-planned and badly-maintained local authority estates. Meanwhile, first-time

Table 1.1 Winners and Losers in the Irish Housing System

Winners	Losers
Speculators and investors	Property-less
Developers and Land owners	Homeless
Financiers (e.g. banks, building societies)	Low income/temporary employed
	Unemployed
Estate agents	Ethnic minorities, those with
Solicitors	disabilities
Landlords	Others in housing need
Home owners	Tenants
Government finances	First-time buyers
Newspaper Property Supplements	

buyers who manage to purchase high-priced housing, even those in relatively well-paid jobs, may in time find that they have taken on unsustainable debt, particularly if interest rates were to increase.

Ireland has the highest rate of house price inflation in the developed world over recent years, and despite the dismissals of lending institutions and other housing-for-profit vested-interest groups, there is evidence to suggest that much Irish housing is significantly 'over-valued'. Consider, for example, that the average price of a loan-purchased new house in Ireland shot up from €72,732 in 1994 to €249,191 in 2004—a staggering increase of 243 per cent. The problem of high house prices is especially evident in the Dublin area, but prospective home-buyers experience difficulty in all our major urban centres. As a result, many opt for home ownership in locations that lack essential social infrastructure and are at considerable distances from the workplace, requiring costly and unsustainable commuting.

Overall, new house prices have risen over four times

faster than house building costs, and seven times faster than the consumer price index since 1994. Had the cost of any other basic necessity skyrocketed in this fashion, it is hard to imagine that there would not have been a far louder public outcry. The many reasons for escalating house prices, which we further consider in Chapter 3, include population growth, higher employment, a lack of alternatives to house purchase, relaxed lending practices by the banks and building societies, and near-monopolistic windfall profits by landowners and property developers. However, a wide range of government policies has also favoured home ownership at the expense of the private rental and public housing sectors, and has, at the very least, helped to facilitate speculation that contributes in turn to increased demand and higher prices. Generous tax incentives over two decades, the absence of a property tax (apart from stamp duty which falls on purchasers) and a reduced capital gains tax have encouraged many players to enter the housing system as investors or speculators, which pits them in direct, not to mention unfair, competition with unfortunate younger first-time buyers. The end result is unsustainable borrowing for the latter and an arguably dangerous level of personal debt for many young people, thanks to the heavy burden of high mortgages.

At the same time, the private rented sector has received less favourable treatment from the state than home owners in Ireland, despite the fact that rents for private housing for most of the past decade have been out of line with the consumer price index and rental trends in other European countries. For example, average rents in Dublin increased by 53 per cent in just three years, from 1998 to 2001. It appears, moreover, that despite a dampening in recent years overall rental increases have tracked house-price increases over the last decade, contributing to the current crisis of rent affordability. A renewed debate on the merits of some form of rent regulation is long overdue. It happens that many middle-class individuals who cannot contemplate house purchase have also become long-term renters, adding to the demand for private accommodation, and creating a "crowding-out" effect that has squeezed the rental market for more economically disadvantaged households.

Unlike our European neighbours, Ireland has made no serious efforts until recently to develop the private rented sector to cater for the obvious needs of tenants. State expenditure on rent supplement (a subsidy paid to private landlords in order to house tenants who cannot afford market rents) has increased from just a few million euro a decade ago to over €350 million. A further €20 million per annum is being spent on emergency bed & breakfast accommodation. It seems obvious that this money could be much better spent in providing permanent accommodation for low-income families. Meanwhile, it remains to be seen whether existing legislation and the new Private Residential Tenancies Act will resolve problems of standards of accommodation and insecurity in the private rented sector that are persistently raised by tenants and their representative organisations. We explore these issues further in Chapter 4.

The difficulties in either purchasing or renting a home at an affordable price has also clearly contributed to the significant increase in the number of families and individuals in need of public housing over the last decade. However, the provision of public housing, either by the local authorities or by housing associations, has unfortunately fallen far short of requirements. We believe the most recent official figure of 48,400 families in housing need seriously underestimates the number who actually require housing, but are not in a position to either purchase or rent at an affordable price. In addition, the urgent needs of marginalised groups—over 5,000 homeless, almost 1,700 Traveller families and thousands more with disabilities—require far more specific attention.

In Chapter 5 we further explore why public housing

provision has failed to keep pace with such needs, despite initiatives such as Part V of the 2000 Planning Act, which was intended to reduce housing segregation by social class – a phenomenon that is particularly obvious in Ireland. We also examine the continuing sale of local authority housing at a discount, at a time when the stock of such housing is so low in relation to need. We similarly take an in-depth look in Chapter 6 at the current vogue, especially in Dublin City Council, for Public-Private Partnerships (PPPs) in order to achieve a 'better mix' of private and public housing. Certainly, the experience to date with a number of flats complexes in Dublin gives cause for serious concern and raises many questions as to whether the handing over of large tracts of land to the private sector in exchange for a relatively modest number of public housing units can be truly justified. At the very least, this experiment needs to be far more transparent, both in relation to the precise costs associated with the projects and the benefits to the local communities involved. And any move by Dublin City Council towards becoming an "enabler" or "facilitator" rather than a direct provider of public housing is particularly worrying in the light of the obvious increased housing needs of the Dublin area.

HOUSING FOR PROFIT OR HOUSING AS A HOME?

The many housing problems in Ireland, and indeed the policies that might help to correct them, depend at the end of the day, upon our philosophical view of housing. Do we see housing as yet another commodity to be bought and sold, or is housing to be regarded first and foremost as shelter and a home – a not-for-profit necessity – and a right to be claimed by all, irrespective of ability to pay?

We argue, and unfortunately so, that housing provision and policy in Ireland have been heavily influenced by the aforementioned market-driven philosophy. The vast brunt of current provision is for sale for profit, or for speculative purposes, a trend that the state has increasingly encouraged in recent years. In the main, housing is perceived and treated both as a commodity like motor cars and race horses, and as a means of wealth creation, like stocks and shares, to be traded on the market. Those with resources or access to credit are able to purchase or rent homes, although increasing numbers do so with considerable difficulty, since there is virtually no control over escalating prices and rents. Even those who are relatively well-off, such as young, two-salaried families, face an uphill struggle, and the overall level of indebtedness arising from these situations remains a matter of serious national concern (Central Bank and Financial Services Authority of Ireland, 2004 and 2005). Furthermore, there is little regulation of the quality of housing in the Irish market sector and no apparent consumer protection. It is also evident that segregation and inequality are integral elements in a market-driven housing system. Those from the lower social classes are excluded or displaced from highly valued residential areas through the prohibitive cost of housing, rapidly escalating land prices and the lack of non-market options. All this, we argue, is the market in action and, as illustrated earlier, it has made big winners of some, done very little for those who have few resources, and made losers of many more.

We can also see our housing-for-profit system in action in the current provision of housing land, a critical and scarce resource, especially in our main urban centres. Nevertheless, land allocation and its price are also left to an imperfect monopolistic market process where relatively few landowners, developers and speculators accumulate land over a period of years and consequently exert considerable control over supply. The re-zoning of land and the granting of planning permission for housing by local authorities are the final mechanisms that deliver large and entirely unearned financial gains for this single privileged group. In the process, the state becomes responsible for the provision of services, such as water, drainage and sewage. Is this "proper planning and development" as required by the Planning Acts? Is this outcome of our market system in the interests of "social justice" and the "common good" as required by the Irish Constitution? We do not believe it is.

When in Chapter 7, we examine housing in a range of European countries and farther afield, we find that market forces can indeed play an important role. We also find, however, that in most countries the market is not generally allowed to dominate to the extent that it has done in Ireland. Throughout Europe, Scandinavia and elsewhere home ownership is certainly encouraged but house price and rent inflation are not, and those who do not have the resources to enter the home ownership or private rental markets are catered for with a variety of innovative measures.

THE IRISH HOUSING SYSTEM: A BRIEF OVERVIEW

We use the term housing system to denote the many elements relevant to the production and allocation of housing, including market and non-market provision, land and labour costs, ownership and rental patterns, finance and policies, as well as its crucial role in social, economic and community development. We start the analysis here with an examination of housing tenures. This brief overview is intended to outline the practical consequences of a dominant market philosophy on three aspects of our housing system—home ownership, private rental and public housing.

Home Ownership
Owning a home has been a long-held aspiration in Ireland and home ownership is now the dominant form of housing tenure. The housing tenure pattern in Ireland since 1961 is

set out in Table 1.2. As far back as 1946, almost 53 per cent of households in Ireland owned a home. By 2002 this proportion had risen to 77 per cent. This pre-occupation with home ownership in Ireland likely derives to some extent from difficult historical experiences and a corresponding high regard for the security attached to property ownership. However, one of the main factors influencing the current high rate of owner-occupation has been a range of government incentives aimed almost exclusively at homeowners, who have been treated far more generously than their counterparts in the private-rented sector over the last four decades. As a result, Ireland at 77 per cent now has one of the highest rates of home ownership in Europe, along with Portugal at 76 per cent, and Italy, Greece and Spain with owner-occupation rates in excess of 80 per cent.

Table 1.2 Occupancy by Tenure, 1961-2002

	1961	1971	1981	1991	2002
000s:					
L A.	124.6	112.6	111.8	98.9	88.2
PRS	116.3	96.7	90.3	81.4	141.5
O/O	404.6	499.7	667.0	808.4	990.7
Other	30.9	17.4	27.0	31.0	59.2
Total	676.4	726.4	896.1	1,019.7	1,279.6
Per Cent:					
L. A.	18.4	15.5	12.5	9.7	6.9
PRS	17.2	13.3	10.1	8.0	11.1
O/O	59.8	68.8	74.4	79.3	77.4
Other	4.6	2.4	3.0	3.0	4.6
Total	100.0	100.0	100.0	100.0	100.0

Source: *Census of Population, 1961-2002*

A number of other new member states of the European Union, namely Hungary, Lithuania and Slovenia also show rates of home ownership in excess of 80 per cent, while Romania and Bulgaria both have a remarkable 97 per cent rate as a result of recent privatisation (Norris and Shiels, 2004).

Private Rental Accomodation

As home ownership has increased in Ireland, the proportion of accommodation provided for rent by private landlords has declined significantly. The privately rented sector, which stood at 26 per cent of the total in 1946, had declined to only 8 per cent by 1991. However, this form of housing tenure expanded to almost 142,000 households by 2002 (an increase of 60,000 in a ten-year period) and now represents 11 per cent of the total. Even if we take into account this recent growth, the Irish figure for privately rented accommodation is quite small compared to most countries in Western Europe or Scandinavia. For example, France, Portugal, and Sweden all have rates of 20 per cent or more, while Austria and Germany have 40 per cent and 51 per cent respectively.

Public Housing

The number of dwellings rented from local authorities in Ireland steadily increased up to 1961 but since then it has dropped consistently – from 125,000 in that year to 88,000 units in 2002. Consequently the Local Authority rental sector now represents a mere 7 per cent of total housing. As with the other housing tenures, the situation with public housing varies considerably throughout Europe –from less than 3 per cent per in Greece, Austria, Spain and Luxembourg to in excess of 20 per cent in the U.K., Denmark and Sweden, with a high of 35 per cent in the Netherlands (Norris and Shiels, 2004).

Market v. Public

In effect, market provision of housing—for profit by the private sector—has been afforded an increasingly dominant role in recent decades, while non-market provision has been greatly reduced. In the past, public provision had played a much more central role, including a substantial public intervention in rural housing from the end of the nineteenth century that amounted to one of the most significant state-subsidised housing programmes at the time in Europe (Fraser, 1996). Moreover, after independence local authorities became increasingly important players in the provision of housing in Dublin and other urban centres, producing good-quality residential environments (MacLaran, 1993, McManus, 2002). From 1932 to 1942 local authorities provided 49,000 units, representing 60 per cent of total housing output. During the Second World War period public provision represented 65 per cent of the housing total and grew as high as 70 per cent in the year 1945/46 (Finnerty, 2002). Even during the early to mid-1950s public provision always exceeded 50 per cent of the total new build. Furthermore, most public housing schemes have been built to a consistently high standard and quality.

Since the late 1950s, however, private provision, normally with state assistance, increased significantly, and by 1975 it represented 67 per cent of the total. Private provision increased further to 93 per cent in 2004 (See Table 1.3), leaving public provision at a mere 7 per cent of the total. This includes a minor role played by housing associations and voluntary bodies, whose contribution on a national basis dropped from 917 in 1996 to just 485 units in 1998 and only recovered to 951 units in 2000 and 1,600 in 2003 and 2004 (Department of Environment, Heritage and Local Government, 2005). In effect, non-market provision has been 'residualised' over many years (Fahey, 1999; Galligan, 1999).

Furthermore, public housing stock has been significantly reduced by a sales policy to tenants at significant discounts of over 230,000 units (out of a stock of approximately 330,000) over the last 70 years. Recent trends highlight this on-going policy of privatisation to which we return later in the book. In any event, the end result is an Ireland now heavily reliant on market provision, where the construction and allocation of housing is mainly left to for-profit providers, and the supply and price of building land is largely unregulated.

Table 1.3 Market and Non-Market Provision of Housing in Ireland

	Market		Non-Market	
	Units	%	Units	%
1975	18,000	67	8,800	33
2004	71,808	93	5,146	7

Source: *Annual Housing Statistics Bulletin*, Various Editions

This current position has been heavily influenced by a strong market philosophy of private ownership, which has pervaded a range of government policies over many years. Not surprisingly, commercial interests supported by the government policies have more recently encouraged a view of housing as a 'product', to be provided and priced by market forces, a view that sees a house more as a means of speculative wealth creation than a necessary shelter and a home. This bias has afforded dominant status to market provision for owner-occupation, de-prioritised public-rental options and further weakened the role of state intervention, whether through direct provision or regulation of the private rental sector. At the same time, an entire range of incentives has been on offer to home owners and private landlords over an extended period. These have included housing grants, mortgage interest tax relief, rates remission, shared ownership and affordable housing schemes, tax breaks and rent subsidies. As mentioned above, an active privatisation programme has also been pursued for many years through the sale of Council housing and land and the recent pre-occupation with Public Private Partnerships in relation to the regeneration of local authority flat complexes.

Finally, many home owners, landlords and those who speculate in housing have managed to pay very little tax. Similarly, those who have owned or speculated in land, especially land close to the main urban centres, have accumulated vast fortunes – sometimes with the collusion of officials and elected representatives in relation to re-zoning and planning permissions. These are among the major winners in our current system. There are, however, significant losers, as we have already detailed, thanks to an abiding inequality built into a housing system whose recent "boom" in price increases has created a crisis of access for so many.

A SUMMARY OF KEY PROBLEMS AND CHALLENGES

Public Housing

- While local authorities and other not-for-profit organisations built 33 per cent of all residences in 1975, this figure had plummeted to 7 per cent by 2004 in spite of the growing need for public housing, exacerbated by soaring house prices.

- Just fewer than 7 per cent of households are now housed by local authorities.

- As the need for social housing steadily grows, local authorities continue to sell off their housing stock at knock-down prices. The result is a modest net gain of only 2,300 units per annum over the last decade.

- The most recent official estimate suggested that 48,400 families (approximately 140,000 people) required social housing in 2002. Our more recent estimate suggests the figure is now considerably higher.

- Over 5,000 people were classified as homeless in 2002.

Private rented sector

- Irish tenants have a long way to go before they reach the conditions enjoyed by many of their European Union counterparts in relation to security of tenure and accommodation standards.

- The plight of tenants in the private rented sector has been largely overlooked. While owner-occupiers, developers and landlords continue to receive substantial tax benefits, private tenants receive very little by way of tax relief or legal protection.

- Ireland recorded the highest level of rent increases in the European Union from 1997 to 2001. Average rents in Dublin increased by 53 per cent from 1998 to 2001, when the consumer price index for the same period rose by only 12 per cent. Some rents fell for a short period up to 2004 but rents have generally begun to increase again.

- The payment of rent supplement to support low-income tenants (in effect a subsidy to private landlords) was intended as a short-term measure that now totals €350 million per annum. A further ad hoc measure—bed & breakfast emergency accommodation for homeless people—is costing €20 million per annum.

House purchase

- Rapidly escalating house prices have pushed home ownership beyond the reach of many, impacting particularly on younger age brackets who contribute dynamically to both the economy and society. Local authority estimates show that 42 per cent of new households in urban areas and 33 per cent nationally will be unable to purchase a home in the immediate future. In Dublin, about half the new households will be unable to purchase a home.

- New house prices have increased over *four* times faster than house building costs and *seven* times faster than the consumer price index since 1994.

- The relaxed lending criteria of Banks and Building Societies contribute to house price inflation and high indebtedness.

- Government policies stimulate demand and thereby fuel further house price inflation.

- Land is a critical resource required for housing. Yet a relatively small group of developers control a high proportion of suitable land for housing, especially in the Dublin region, which allows for windfall profits and a near-monopoly in the entire area of housing sales and building land.

In view of the multiple problems identified, we would argue that housing can no longer be treated simply as a market commodity or "get-rich-quick" speculative opportunity. Rather a house needs to recapture its traditional role as a social good and its universal status as a fundamental human right. In order to achieve this, policies must be implemented to ensure that every person has affordable, secure, good quality accommodation appropriate to their needs. To that end a number of key principles and proposed policy changes are explored in our concluding chapter.

CONCLUSION

The degree to which any government can effectively deal with these difficult challenges depends on the philosophical position which it embraces. The strong market orientation that has recently emerged in our housing system is itself the result of an on-going shift in the relative influence of public, private, philanthropic and voluntary players over many decades. This shift has happened for a number of reasons, political, economic, cultural, social, and ideological, but the consequent predominance of market influences has meant uneven consequences for different sectors of society, creating a clear division between winners and losers, and a growing social crisis that only resolute government action can resolve.

If we fail to act, further persistent and significant house price increases, tracked closely by private rents, could impede if not seriously compromise the considerable economic progress achieved in Ireland over the last decade. Continuing exceptional increases will inevitably give rise to significant wage demands and inflation, as evidenced by recent demands in the building industry and concerns expressed by Trade Union leaders, the Small Firms Association, the Irish Central Bank, the OECD and the IMF. Indeed, the generally favourable international perception of Ireland's economy could be irrevocably damaged, if serious action is not taken as a matter of urgency.

Yet such serious action, we believe, also requires us to re-examine the collection of received beliefs, assumptions, and theories that underpin the dominant role of the market in our housing system. We turn to this issue in Chapter 2.

Chapter 2

Housing Systems: A Question of Philosophy

The fundamental need for shelter is well captured in Pádraic Colum's beautiful poem where the old woman, tired and weary of years of homelessness, yearns to have "a little house – a house of her own – out of the wind and the rain's way". Even in the developed world, thousands, whether in rural or urban areas, have inadequate accommodation or none at all. Worse still, millions in the developing countries of Africa, South America and Asia have little hope of ever having a secure home appropriate to their needs. This is surely unacceptable in the twenty first century in a world of incredible economic progress, vast wealth and technological virtuosity. It cries out for action.

A great deal has been said and written about housing over the last fifteen years. A comprehensive review and critique of housing policy was produced by the late John Blackwell for the National Economic and Social Council in 1988 (Blackwell, 1988). Ten years later detailed overviews of the housing problem and an evaluation of housing policy were produced by Downey (1998) and O'Sullivan (1999). Three Reports commissioned by the Government were produced by Peter Bacon and Associates dealing almost exclusively with owner-occupied housing (Bacon, 1998, 1999 and 2000). A study on social housing and its management has been published (Fahey, 1999). The four Dublin Local Authorities published a set of recommendations relating to housing in the Dublin area (Dublin Local Authorities, 1999). An independent Housing Commission (Drudy et al. 1999) and the National Economic and Social Forum (NESF, 2000) also published detailed assessments. A government-commissioned Report appeared on the privately rented sector (Commission on the Private Rented Residential Sector, 2000) as did an important study by McCashin (2000). A comparative study of Northern Ireland and the Republic of Ireland was published by Paris (2001). Four voluntary agencies carried out a detailed study of housing access (Punch et al. 2002). Most recently, the National Economic and Social Council produced a further report examining the nature of the housing problem and suggesting policy changes (NESC, 2004). During this period numerous other papers and reviews have appeared in books and academic journals. We draw on many of these throughout this book.

What has been the result of all of this analysis of this central issue? There is no doubt that some progress has been made since the 1988 NESC Report, although many of the concerns raised by John Blackwell and the NESC Council remain unresolved (McCashin and Brooke, 2005). A considerable number of houses and apartments have been constructed for sale or for rent. Basic facilities which were lacking several decades ago are now generally available. Many people have benefited. Some individuals and families even own second homes in Ireland and in other countries. Some individuals and companies, whether as investors or speculators, own multiple properties. The construction industry is a significant employer. Despite this, a substantial minority of our population are no nearer to owning a home or renting one at an affordable price than they were ten years ago. Furthermore, the waiting list for local authority housing has increased, and there is a persistent problem of homelessness suffered by the most vulnerable people in our society, despite excellent work by agencies such as Focus Ireland, the Iveagh Trust, the Homeless Agency, the Simon Communities of Ireland, Trust, Arrupe and others. The high economic and employment growth rates during the 1990s and since then have done little to alleviate these difficulties; indeed they may have exacerbated them. This is a matter of great concern. Furthermore, our failure to date to provide adequate affordable housing appropriate to need for all people is one of the key obstacles towards reducing the significant inequalities which persist in Irish society.

Why have we failed so far to resolve the housing problem for a considerable number of our people? Have central and local government policy initiatives been too weak? Are our people unwilling to accept the need for serious change and are our politicians fearful of initiating such change? We believe that policy initiatives have indeed been largely ad hoc and weak due to the (perhaps correct) perception that the voting public will punish any government proposing fundamental change. For example, those who currently own their homes – many after a considerable struggle – are in the majority, representing about 77 per cent of the total. Many of these perhaps regard themselves as "asset rich" and may not be particularly concerned about the escalation of house prices – indeed some may uncritically applaud such inflation. Neither are they overly concerned by the level of rents charged by private landlords, by the conditions of much private rented accommodation or by lengthening local authority waiting lists.

We would suggest that a central part of our problem is that we have, over the years, accepted a type of philosophy that is not really appropriate for such a fundamental necessity as a home. In recent years, housing analysis and policy in Ireland have been under-pinned by a dominant paradigm and philosophy which sees "the market" as the ideal provider and allocator of housing. This approach seeks to minimise the direct provision of housing by the state; rather it asserts that the state's role is to facilitate such provision by private developers, to fast-track planning permissions and re-zonings and to encourage private provision with tax and other incentives, while carrying the cost of essential services such as water, sewage, roads and amenities. While public housing is still provided by Local Authorities and other non-profit organisations, this is on a modest scale and the market approach to provision is now the dominant one in Ireland.

We believe that housing problems and inequality – whether in Ireland or elsewhere – are linked to a particular kind of housing system shaped by a broader "paradigm" or set of received beliefs and characterised by its philosophical emphasis, policy orientation and practical priorities. We employ the term "paradigm" with purpose, in line with Thomas Kuhn's (1957, 1962) ideas, to capture this complexity. While in any given historic phase, certain political philosophies, practical priorities and powerful interest groups influence and shape social and economic policies, alternative views, approaches and challenges always exist and invariably come to displace the older ways. Thus, it is important to evaluate the nature of the current dominant paradigm in housing, as well as its philosophical basis and its social, economic and environmental consequences for different groups and localities. In the light of this, there may be a case for constructing an alternative paradigm. We contend that all of this matters in a most urgent way given the fundamental importance of housing and accommodation to people's well-being, dignity and to community and societal development.

MARKET OR NON-MARKET: COMMODITY OR HOME

Housing systems vary in critical ways, reflecting their long and complex evolution and embeddedness in the general development trajectory of a particular country or region (with its own complexities and variations in terms of socio-economic structure, political ideology and inequality). A number of commentators have suggested that housing systems have certain key features which in turn present important and challenging philosophical and policy questions.

One particularly critical feature relates to the 'content' or 'tendencies' within various housing systems in terms of their 'market' and 'non-market' elements. This is because, in some respects, different housing systems are characterised above all by a particular articulation of 'market' and 'non-market' policies, which focuses respectively on whether housing is treated as a commodity or a home. In this section, we offer a summary framework to develop this distinction. It should be stressed that contemporary housing systems in Europe and elsewhere contain both market and non-market tendencies; the degree to which either tendency is emphasised and supported is one of the key factors underpinning the considerable variation between housing systems over time and space.

At one extreme, the housing system is strongly commodified, relying largely on the 'market' forces of supply and demand to allocate and determine the price or rent of housing. If there is excess supply, developers, builders, landlords and estate agents will have empty houses for sale or rent and prices are likely to fall as a result. Those seeking homes will benefit from an increased choice and lower prices. On the other hand, excess demand will tend to push up prices and rents and put purchasers under pressure. Prices will tend to settle (or reach 'equilibrium') when supply equals demand. In theory, this is the way the 'housing market' should operate. There are of course a whole range of markets, depending on differences in age, architecture, size and location. In a properly functioning market, prices would be relatively stable due to competition between many sellers and buyers. However, this is rarely, if ever, the case.

There is a further problem. In a market, one can secure exactly as many "housing commodities" as can be paid for, but on a low or insecure income, this may amount to very little and may result in procuring poor housing or none at all. Thus, there is an important distinction between the social concept of "need" and the economic concept of "market demand". The term demand refers to the willingness of consumers to purchase or rent products or services at certain prices but, most important of all, it also implies ability to pay those prices. Those involved in the production or sale of housing do so in order to earn incomes or profits. Housing will not be provided to those who cannot pay – to do so is beyond the logic of the market. The term demand should not therefore be confused with the term 'need' which indicates a need or requirement for housing, but does not necessarily mean that the person in need has the ability to pay. Given the broad household-income variations between different classes, gender and ethnic groups, it is obvious that the 'market' must exclude a whole range of individuals who have not the ability to pay. Nevertheless, this commodification of housing is applauded as an 'ideal' or 'natural' mechanism by many economists, developers, estate agents, landlords and those representing the building industry.

At the other extreme, the housing system may be decommodified to a large extent, emphasising non-market not-for-profit provision. It caters for those who are in need of housing, but may be unwilling or unable to enter the housing market. In this case, providers of housing have motives other than procuring income or profit. Normally, non-market provision is encouraged and facilitated by central and local government as well as by various voluntary and philanthropic bodies, but the role of such housing and its extent and quality varies significantly between different housing systems. In some countries there is an important tradition of individual or community self-build models, and the co-operative housing movement is also strong in some cases. In many decommodified housing systems, the production process would of course still be dominated by builders who make a profit from construction. Although there may be in this case a 'construction profit', the speculative gains characteristic of commodified systems are reduced or even eliminated (Barlow and Duncan, 1994).

HOUSING AS A COMMODITY: SOME PECULIARITIES

In the case of market provision, housing is regarded as a 'commodity' like any other commodity such as televisions or motor cars. Certain characteristics follow from this 'commodification' of housing. Thus, it is produced in order to make a profit. The main contribution of housing is then measured in *quantitative* terms (levels of profit, return on investment, capital gain), while its real *qualitative* essence (as shelter, home, place in community development) is a secondary consideration. It follows, therefore, that the acquisition of a house depends above all on ability to pay. In the case of housing for purchase, this normally means the ability to borrow a substantial sum of money from a building society or bank. A number of factors will determine the ability to borrow, including well-paid and steady employment, the ownership of other property, or access to relations who are prepared to protect the lender by acting as guarantor or by providing informal 'loans' to cover deposits or other costs. In effect, those on low incomes normally fail to fulfill these 'requirements' and are therefore excluded from competing for housing in the market. On the other hand, those on high incomes will be the main participants and beneficiaries in the market (Drudy and Punch, 2002).

Furthermore, in line with market 'ideologies', those producing or selling tend to urge purchase on the grounds that 'it is a good investment' and 'will appreciate in value', particularly if it is located in a 'good area'. When property prices are rising rapidly, aspiring purchasers are urged to 'buy now before prices rise further'. Those who already own property are advised (and think) that they are 'sitting on a goldmine', and they may be encouraged to further improve their position by becoming multiple home-owners in the expectation of a secure return on such investment. As with stocks and shares, 'profit-taking' is an inevitable and much-sought element in the process.

A further critical element in the commodification process is the acquisition of land by private individuals or developers, sometimes over a long period of years, enabling them to exert considerable control over the production and prices of housing. The availability of land is a prerequisite for the provision of housing and therefore those who own or control it can exercise what has been called a 'double monopoly' (Yamada, 1999). First, there is obviously a relatively fixed supply of land. Second, land for housing depends on the willingness of landowners to release and sell for such purposes. When there is excess demand for housing, the inevitable outcome is an upward pressure on the price of land. The 're-zoning' or granting of planning permission by the state can often exacerbate this price escalation further, resulting in large 'unearned' gains derived from land ownership. If this occurs, it invariably feeds into the eventual price of housing for sale or rent.

It can also be argued that the operation of the housing market tends to encourage the 'segregation' of housing types and particular social groups. As mentioned above, those providing and selling houses rely on a standard formula which suggests that, apart from being a home, a house is good value for money, a sensible and secure investment and an appreciating asset which can be 'traded up' or from which 'profit-taking' can take place at any time. In order to protect these suggested attributes as well as the all-important 'location', it becomes important to avoid dilution of the product with low-priced homes or those from lower socio-economic groups or otherwise defined as 'undesirables'. The market can play a central role in such segregation, particularly at a time of rising prices. The basic process at work here is essentially similar to "gentrification" (Smith, 1996), whereby those from the lower social classes are excluded or displaced from the highly valued areas through the prohibitive cost of housing, rapidly escalating land prices and the lack of non-market options. These elite residential areas are thereby ring-fenced from invasion by the poor or other 'undesirable' social groups, who must then seek accommodation elsewhere. Thus, the commodification of housing is also a central force in residential differentiation, that is, the creation of socially distinct areas – from ghettos to élite enclaves.

HOUSING AS A HOME – A DEVELOPMENT PERSPECTIVE

For the majority of people the most important immediate meaning attached to housing is as a home – shelter, a place to stay, to feel secure, build a base, find an identity, participate in a community and society. Housing thus becomes a central feature of "development" – a process not simply comprising increases in economic growth, but containing positive actions to improve the quality of life and well-being for all (Todaro and Smith, 2005). Taking such a perspective, we would prioritise such concerns from the outset. Here, housing would be treated primarily as a 'social good' like education or public health and would be produced mainly in response to need as well as the ability to pay. This perspective is in fact quite common and housing is given the status of a 'right' in the Constitution or legislation in some countries.

We would therefore argue that it is essential to place housing in a broader "development" framework. This idea is gaining increasing acceptance. The basic point is that people need homes, but their needs (and their demands) will not be met by the provision of housing alone. A better quality of life and well-being for all are the real measures of whether or not real development takes place in any society. These will be achieved only when, in addition to a secure affordable dwelling appropriate to needs, a more comprehensive set of related needs and requirements are satisfied. These include access to appropriate employment opportunities, better education and lifelong learning, a high standard of health and nutrition, less poverty, greater equality, a cleaner environment as well as sufficient social and cultural amenities (Todaro and Smith, 2005). This development perspective is a prerequisite for good housing policy. It places the emphasis on "human development", "human rights", inclusiveness and sustainability as well as on having appropriate institutions and values which put people and life to the forefront. As Korten puts it:

> At its core, the root cause of our collective crisis is two fold: a failure of our values and a failure of our institutions. We have created a global culture that values money and materialism over life itself. In our pursuit of money we have given the institutions of money – banks, investment houses, financial markets, and publicly traded corporations – the power to rule over life. Recognizing only financial values, accountable only for money's replication, and wholly unmindful of the needs of life, these institutions are wantonly destroying life to make money. It's a bad bargain (Korten, 1998)

The common thread running through these various approaches is that we need to focus explicitly on outcomes. This means, for example, turning attention to questions about inequality (who benefits and who loses) rather than just focusing on the mechanisms of economic activity and growth, and it must also encourage greater concern for the development of people and societies rather than an inherent emphasis on production for the sake of production.

This line of argument has several implications for how we think about (and respond to) housing questions. For one, it directs us back to the core principle that shelter is a basic human need, of direct importance to quality of life and well-being – a central element of development. Everybody has a legitimate need of housing, and the central challenge for policy is to ensure that this need is met for all – and it becomes the right of all – in an appropriate, affordable and sustainable manner. There are of course many different kinds of household with different types and levels of housing need – lone parents, elderly, disabled, single people, women and children – so that the housing system needs to be diverse and flexible as well as accessible (see, for example, O'Sullivan, 2002; Brooke, 2004).

The question of inequality is thus central to any consideration of need and development. The uneven development of economies and societies generates patterns of advantage and disadvantage, privilege and marginalisation, winning and losing groups, across every geographic scale, global, national, regional and local. This is reflected in a range of disparities between different regions and places (signalled in a variety of popular spatial metaphors – north/south, first world/third world, core/periphery, ghetto/enclave) and social groups (class, ethnic, racial, gender divisions).

This leads us to a whole range of critical social issues in housing regarding inequality and the differential distribution of or access to decent accommodation (Lee et al., 1995; Forrest and Murie, 1995; Lee and Murie, 1997; Drudy and Punch, 2001; Fitzgerald and Winston, 2005). Households who are economically vulnerable and disempowered in the first instance may often be further disadvantaged within the housing system, though good housing policies might counteract this or even act as a progressive mechanism of income redistribution. Others face difficulties due to their "special" needs (i.e. legitimate social needs to which the housing system does not respond well), including those of the elderly, those with disabilities, refugees, asylum seekers, homeless people, leaving institutions, ethnic minorities, including travellers. It is worth reminding ourselves, however, that the term "special" needs (with the implication that households in other social situations have "normal" needs) is questionable. Everyone has a need for housing, though the specific housing solution (or housing problem) will vary quite a bit. The real issue is that the more comprehensive set of housing-related needs often receive insufficient attention :

> ...for those who need support in their housing, unfortunately, the model runs out of steam quickly. It appears that once the bricks, mortar and price are surpassed as elements of adequate housing, there is a gap in the conceptual framework of pure housing policy. Anything which involves a design matter outside the standard house type, or which involves any agency other than builder, lender and solicitor, is deemed a special needs case (Kenna, 2001: 8).

In short, there is a range of needs to which the housing system, as currently configured, does not respond well.

Thus, there are very different possible answers to the question "what is housing?" These two opposite understandings lead to contrasting policy priorities, as illustrated by the simplified framework provided in Table 2.1, which attempts to illustrate a range of possible meanings and characteristic features of housing systems.

FINDING THE BALANCE?

A key point running through this discussion is that these

market and non-market tendencies cannot be viewed in isolation; rather they represent opposite poles in a continuum of possible configurations, which may characterise any housing system. It is important to realise, for instance, that there is no such thing as a 'perfect' market in housing: state intervention and regulation are invariably present and are essential requirements. The important question, however, is the philosophical orientation of such intervention (tending to promote or reduce commodification, for instance) and the priorities or dominant emphasis in the practical policies implemented.

Table 2.1 Housing as Commodity vs. Housing as Home

Housing as a Commodity	Housing as a home
←	→
Market Provision	Non-market provision
Commodity for sale	Housing as a right for shelter
Housing as an economic good	Housing as a merit good
Demand/ability to pay	Housing linked to needs
Developer/Speculator profits	Non profit or construction
Personal investment/profit	profit only
taking, wealth generation	Home, community, shelter, etc.
Speculative acquisition of land	Public land banking for
& capital gains; monopolies	building and provision
Segregation	Integration

For example, the availability of sufficient and suitable serviced land is central to the provision of all housing, whether provided and allocated by the market mechanism or through public land banking. In the case of land, the state can exert considerable control over market providers by a range of regulations and policies on rezoning, planning permission and taxation policies. At the same time, non-market provision may also involve input by private-sector players, particularly builders or construction companies. In countries where non-market housing is sold off by the state, this category can quickly take on market characteristics, since it becomes available for 'trading up' and 'profit-taking'. Where public land banking is not implemented in a serious way, non-market providers may also have to compete in the open market for sites, a factor that may severely compromise their ability to have a significant impact. The state may also adopt different positions with regard to the protection and level of support afforded different interests in the housing system – tenants, owners, private developers, land owners, non-profit providers, and so on. A key consideration in this context is the level of protection afforded to private property rights over the general interests of the wider community and society i.e., the common good.

These different tendencies present a policy and philosophical question of critical importance: is the first priority of a housing system the realisation of investment, speculative or capital gains for those with the necessary resources or the realisation of housing as a home and the right of all citizens? Different countries have adopted different balances or philosophical orientations and resulting policies. In some cases, housing has been strongly commodified through an emphasis on market provision and the residualisation of social provision, while other states have taken a more balanced approach.

This leaves us with a number of questions. To begin with, the first problem is to establish what is the particular philosophical and policy orientation in a given housing system at a particular period in time. A subsequent challenge is to evaluate the social, economic and environmental impact or outcomes of the system on various groups – home-owners as well as private and public tenants or those aspiring to these categories. Who are the winners and losers in the system? Are we as a society satisfied with the operation and impact of the system or do we need to propose changes? In order to make progress, we need to devise some basic principles, which might guide us in defining a "good" housing system or paradigm. While it may be difficult to get universal agreement on this, as a starting point we present here some simple principles which seem important to us.

PRINCIPLES FOR A GOOD HOUSING PARADIGM

- We would suggest, first and foremost, that housing which is affordable and appropriate to needs should be available to all as a basic *human right*. This is because shelter is a basic human need, and housing is absolutely central to human, community and societal development – to be without a home compromises people's dignity and many other crucial aspects of life, including health, employment, education and other critical needs.

- The housing system needs to be a central element of a *sustainable development* strategy. A key issue here is that the housing system should not compromise the possibilities for future as well as present generations. It would also entail careful advance planning of various land uses, transport, amenities and services for residential development. It means adopting a sound urban, regional and local development strategy, one that creates a balanced spatial pattern of economic and social activities with integral links between land use, transport, social services, amenities and economic activities. It needs to operate in line with sound ecological principles and with full respect for the safeguarding and enhancement of the natural and social environment.

- The principles of *social justice* and *the common good* should be central in relation to land ownership and residential development. The housing paradigm should be *inclusive and participative,* since a system that encourages segregation, exclusive development, and the denial of housing access to particular groups is seriously compromised. People instead need to be empowered to have effective choices and to have a real influence over their broader residential and social environments. This imperative means encouraging community-development models of housing management and fostering a sense of local identity and ownership where possible. Authoritarian or paternalistic models of housing management of the past would thus be eliminated.

- The housing system needs to operate in a manner that is *fair*. It would provide even-handed treatment for the various housing tenures and the groups within them – a tenure neutral system. This also means eliminating discrimination, whether on grounds of class, ethnicity, race, age, gender or other distinctions. It means ensuring that people have a fair chance to secure appropriate housing that is suitable to needs and affordable so that they can take a real part in their communities and in broader society and can find the security to develop all of their capacities and potential and live a full life. Thus, we need to start to view (and evaluate) housing systems in terms of quality of life rather than solely in economic or quantitative terms (i.e. in terms of so many units produced or so much wealth created or capital gains).

The above list is not of course exhaustive, but we would hope that it might serve to encourage an integrated rather than a divided housing system. That is, one that operates in a fair manner built on the principles of sustainability, inclusiveness, participation, equality, social justice, the common good and with full recognition and respect for economic, social and cultural rights.

CONCLUSION

As stated already, we believe that market ideologies have become the dominant forces underlying recent policy evolution in Ireland. This is, of course, a global tendency, evident across different societies: the process of emphasising market strategies as the ideal mechanism for organising not just economic relations but also social policies and many areas of life and development. One could call this the "business model" of society, built on an economic paradigm that emphasises individualism, growth, accumulation and even greed rather than a more "holistic development" model which focuses on the quality of life and all that this entails.

Under the influence of market ideologies, the housing system has become increasingly commodified, tipping the balance towards market and away from non-market policies and concerns. It is not intended to imply in a simplistic manner that housing policies have been completely taken over by free-market ideologies. However, the outcomes of a number of recent policy initiatives, explored in subsequent chapters, as well as the general realignment of the Irish housing system over the course of recent decades, could reasonably be interpreted in this way, suggesting the predominant influence of a commodified philosophy of housing.

If the dominant housing paradigm at any time is the result of definite philosophical and ideological positions that currently hold sway, the influence of that same body of assumptions and beliefs can also ebb and flow, depending on both the government in power and the influence of the most powerful interest groups in land and housing – including landowners, property developers, builders and lending institutions. These are key interest groups in Ireland today and their influence with government is considerable. These are also important factors in the "market" shift in housing. In this approach, the market is king, housing is a commodity, speculation and profit-taking are the norm, and inequality is perpetuated. Indeed, housing inequality is in fact not an unfortunate by-product but arguably an integral component of the market system. The outcome is most likely to be a divided housing system.

CHAPTER 3

The Market in Action: A Home at a Price

Owning a home has been a long-held aspiration in Ireland. However, as we show in this chapter, there are many problems associated with purchasing a home. Before examining these, it is important to point out that the problems of purchasing a home are inextricably linked to the situation in other housing tenures – private rental and public housing which we deal with in later chapters. For example, high house prices and affordability are in part the result of a lack of alternatives to house purchase. Despite an increase in the number of private rental units in recent years, there are still insufficient to meet the demand. Accordingly, renting a home in the private rental sector has been, and remains, costly. Tax relief available to tenants has been modest in comparison with that available to home owners. Private rental has also proved an insecure tenure and until recently tenants could be ordered to leave without explanation at 28 days notice. Furthermore, much of the private rented accommodation has been and continues to be of low standard and very little has been done to rectify this problem over many years. There has, therefore, been every incentive for individuals and families to get out of this sector and, if possible, to avail of the better incentives associated with owner occupation.

The other alternative to purchasing a home is to rent one from the Local Authority or from a Housing Association. Traditionally, such accommodation has been relatively cheap and over many years has played a central role in providing housing for those who cannot afford to either purchase or rent on the private market. With the significant increase in waiting lists, many give up on this option. Of course, low income families have no other choice and must hold on in the hope of eventually securing a home. In any event, the critical point is that there are currently few viable alternatives to purchasing a home for many individuals and families. This means that the demand increases for homes for sale on the private market, thus putting an upward pressure on house prices. If, on the other hand, there were sufficient good quality, affordable private rental and social housing units available, many families would avail of these options, thus postponing any bid for home ownership and reducing demand and prices accordingly. It is essential that policy makers should fully appreciate these critical links between the various tenures.

ESCALATING HOUSE PRICES AND AFFORDABILITY

Over the last ten years accelerating house prices have created a major difficulty of "affordability", especially for first-time buyers. House purchase is now simply beyond the reach of a significant number of people, even those on relatively high incomes. But how can we assess what is affordable? Some commentators, and especially those involved in the building industry, estate agents and lending institutions will inevitably suggest that housing is as affordable as ever. On the other hand, a number of indicators can be used to show that this is not the case. What do members of households themselves think? One recent survey certainly showed that Irish households perceive that they have housing costs above the European average. In the survey, 19.5 per cent of Irish households stated that costs were burdensome compared with only 4.8 per cent of households in the Netherlands and 6.8 per cent in Denmark (Healy, 2004). Certainly many couples with two average incomes are unable to bridge the gap between the recommended Central Bank loan maximum (2.5 times the first income plus the second income) and the house price. As an example (using the average new house price for 2004) even if a couple earned €30,000 each (i.e. each at the average industrial wage), the traditional maximum loan would be €105,000, leaving a shortfall of €217,000 in Dublin. Similarly, the shortfall would be €137,000 in Galway, €132,000 in Cork, €115,000 in Waterford and €106,000 in Limerick. This recommended loan/income guideline has therefore been consistently ignored as lending agencies receive "comfort" from parents or other relations who provide deposits and "guarantees" to protect the lender in the event of default. Unfortunately, these actions have contributed to continued price inflation and potentially unsustainable borrowing.

Before examining a number of affordability indicators let us look at the way new house prices have increased over the past few decades. The new house price changes since 1974 are given in Fig. 3.1 (see also Appendix A1). While prices rose fairly consistently since 1974, the major escalation only commenced about 1994/95. When we adjust for inflation we find that a significant price rise occurred for a brief period in the late 1970s but prices fell back and remained virtually static throughout the 1980s until 1994/95. Second-hand house prices showed similar increases since 1994 (Fig. 3.2) from which our current problem dates.

The average new house price for which loans were approved for the country as a whole increased from €72,732 in 1994 to €249,191 in 2004 – an increase of 243 per cent. Over the same period, the average new house price in

Figure 3.1 New House Prices in Dublin and Ireland, 1974–2004

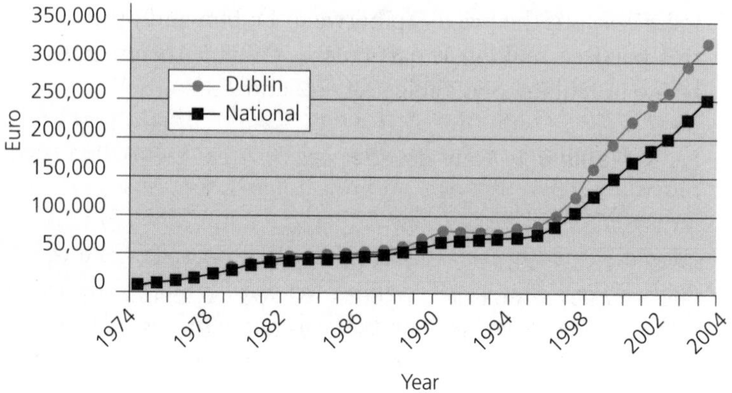

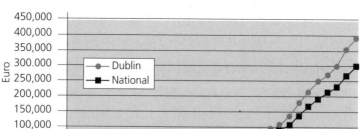

Source: *Annual Housing Statistics Bulletin*, various editions

Figure 3.2 Second-Hand House Prices in Dublin and Ireland, 1974–2004

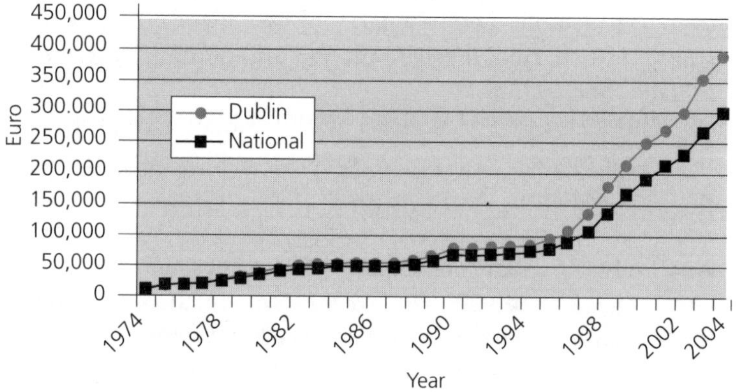

Source: *Annual Housing Statistics Bulletin*, various editions

Dublin increased from €81,993 to €322,628 or 296 per cent. The average second-hand house price for the country as a whole increased from €69,877 in 1994 to €294,667 in 2004 – an increase of 322 per cent. Over the same period, the average second hand house price in Dublin increased from

€82,772 to €389,791 or 371 per cent. Most other urban centres of the country have also experienced significant increases, but the price gap between Dublin and other centres persists, making it particularly difficult to purchase a home in Dublin. See Tables 3.1, 3.2 and 3.3.

Table 3.1 New House Prices by Area, 1994-2004 (€s)

	State	Dublin	Cork	Galway	Limerick	Waterford	Other areas
1994	72,732	81,993	71,378	77,375	68,238	69,185	66,829
1995	77,994	86,671	76,608	87,783	73,348	69,950	71,829
1996	87,202	97,058	85,351	93,050	83,281	79,784	82,091
1997	102,222	122,036	96,046	109,905	91,077	91,608	94,664
1998	125,302	160,699	112,133	118,738	104,248	107,954	116,589
1999	148,521	193,526	141,007	138,928	121,880	132,050	136,970
2000	169,191	221,724	166,557	163,824	145,834	145,713	154,050
2001	182,863	243,095	174,550	171,161	152,205	155,488	166,834
2002	198,087	256,109	184,369	187,607	168,574	167,272	179,936
2003	224,567	291,646	211,980	223,388	197,672	195,173	203,125
2004	249,191	322,628	237,858	242,218	210,868	220,286	228,057

Source: *Annual Housing Statistics Bulletin*, various editions

Table 3.2 Second-Hand House Prices by Area, 1994-2004 (€s)

	State	Dublin	Cork	Galway	Limerick	Waterford	Other areas
1994	69,877	82,772	63,883	69,258	58,405	55,347	61,567
1995	74,313	88,939	70,796	78,370	61,099	59,409	64,170
1996	85,629	104,431	77,152	88,020	71,066	62,956	74,254
1997	102,712	131,258	88,535	100,791	78,256	73,308	86,347
1998	134,529	176,420	110,432	126,914	96,791	93,948	111,878
1999	163,316	210,610	139,473	147,152	119,072	115,768	135,096
2000	190,550	247,039	169,064	166,145	142,188	141,662	158,442
2001	206,117	267,939	179,687	189,713	157,176	155,242	177,203
2002	227,799	297,424	200,155	206,571	172,273	170,342	192,301
2003	264,898	355,451	240,444	249,404	201,477	201,871	218,061
2004	294,667	389,791	273,605	278,813	218,869	220,029	235,829

Source: *Annual Housing Statistics Bulletin*, various editions

Table 3.3 Annual Percentage Increase in New House Prices in Ireland, 1994-2004

	State	Dublin	Cork	Galway	Limerick	Waterford	Other Areas
1994-95	7.2	5.7	7.3	13.5	7.5	1.1	7.5
1995-96	11.8	12.0	11.4	6.0	13.5	14.1	14.3
1996-97	17.2	25.7	12.5	18.1	9.4	13.2	15.3
1997-98	22.6	31.7	16.7	8.0	14.5	19.5	23.2
1998-99	18.5	20.4	25.7	17.0	16.9	22.3	17.5
1999-00	13.9	14.5	18.1	17.9	19.7	10.3	12.5
2000-01	8.1	9.6	4.8	4.5	4.3	6.7	8.3
2001-02	8.3	5.4	5.6	9.6	10.8	7.6	7.9
2002-03	13.4	13.9	15.4	16.1	19.2	17.5	12.9
2003-04	11.0	10.6	12.2	8.4	6.7	12.9	12.3

Source: *Annual Housing Statistics Bulletin,* various editions

It is readily apparent that there have been exceptional price increases over the period since 1994. How do these increases compare with other commonly-used price indices? See Fig. 3.3. Up to 1994, new house prices increased broadly in line with the Consumer Price Index, house building costs (comprising labour and material costs) and average industrial earnings. Since 1994, however, house prices have diverged significantly from these other indices. Using a base of 1991 = 100, house building costs (labour and materials) increased from 111 in 1994 to 180 in 2004 or 62 per cent. The Consumer Price Index increased from 108 to 146 or 35 per cent. Over the same period, the index for new house prices for the country as a whole increased from 109 to 372, or 241 per cent. In other words, new house prices have increased about four times faster than house building costs and average earnings and almost seven times faster than the consumer price index since 1994. If any other necessity rose in price to such an extent, there would have been a public outcry.

It may be noted that after accelerating in the late 1990s, there was a dampening down in the rate of increase in new

Figure 3.3 New House Prices, Earnings, Building Costs, CPI, 1994–2004

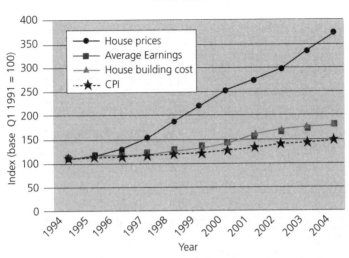

Source: *Annual Housing Statistics Bulletin,* various editions

house prices (to less than 10 per cent) from 2000 to 2002 (see Table 3.3), although the absolute increases involved were still substantial. However, the following year (2002-03) house prices accelerated again, especially in Dublin, Limerick, Waterford and Galway, with little change in 2004 or during 2005. For the most recent available data for the year up to June 2005, new house prices for the country as a whole rose by 12 per cent, and by 17 per cent and 16 per cent in Cork and Galway respectively. Even in Dublin where the percentage increase was 7 per cent, the *absolute* increase was substantial and it is these increases (in thousands of euro) that are of critical concern to those contemplating the purchase of a home. As shown in Table 3.4 average new house prices in the year to June 2005 rose by €29,000 for the country as a whole, by €23,800 in Dublin (from an already high base), by €38,400 in Galway and by €39,600 in Cork. Furthermore, average house prices in rural areas, small towns and villages (the "other areas" category) increased by 12 per cent or €27,000 in this

Table 3.4   New House Prices by Area,
June 2004 – June 2005

	State	Dublin	Cork	Galway	Limerick	Waterford	Other areas
June 04	246,299	322,899	229,341	244,074	210,095	227,363	225,083
Sep 04	249,348	324,304	236,719	233,180	207,984	217,176	231,217
Dec 04	262,277	329,447	252,726	261,304	221,725	223,067	239,209
March 05	264,472	342,304	255,027	265,291	213,717	238,619	242,197
June 05	275,394	346,683	268,938	282,475	220,321	233,445	252,075
Absolute Annual Change	29,095	23,784	39,597	38,401	10,226	6,082	26,992

Source: *Annual Housing Statistics Bulletin*, various editions

most recent period. These changes show clearly that the escalation in house prices is continuing.

It should be emphasised that the average prices given above conceal major variations between different areas and in different housing markets. For example, there was some astonishment a few years ago when €1 million houses on relatively small sites went on sale in a number of exclusive areas of Dublin and there was no shortage of wealthy buyers. Indeed, in 2005 most homes in parts of our capital city would carry close to this price tag. The weekly much-enlarged property supplements in *the Irish Times, Irish Independent, Sunday Tribune* and *Sunday Business Post* regularly report private treaty and auction sales of several million euro and more for individual and, it might be said, unexceptional homes. Suburban homes with substantial gardens or corner sites have become particularly popular with property investors, speculators and builders who are more than willing to comply with, or even exceed, the new "densification" guidelines issued by the Department of the Environment, Heritage and Local Government and the Local Authorities.

But let us return to the dramatic increases in new house

prices over the last decade. How do these price increases compare with the situation in other countries? Drawing on an index of house prices published by *The Economist* magazine in June 2005 we find that over the period 1997-2005, Ireland had the highest rate of price increase (192 per cent) of all the relatively developed countries examined. It was followed by Britain (154 per cent), Spain (145 per cent), and Australia (114 per cent). Most countries were well below these figures. For example, the United States, New Zealand and Canada increased by 73 per cent, 66 per cent and 47 per cent respectively. A number of countries even registered negative rates; thus house prices in Hong Kong fell by 43 per cent during the period examined, Japan by 28 per cent and Germany by 0.2 per cent. In the light of this survey, *The Economist* argued that Irish housing was significantly "overvalued" and it predicted a drop in house prices over the next few years. There is certainly little doubt that Irish house prices are out of line with normal inflationary tendencies as shown above. We give in Table 3.5 an indication of how house prices would have changed if they had, over the period 1994-2004, risen at the same rate as the building cost index, average earnings and the consumer price index. Table 3.5 shows clearly that, had they done so, house prices would be much lower than they are today. In any event, house prices appear to us to be well above what we might reasonably expect them to be. They are indeed significantly "overvalued" or, more accurately, over-priced.[1]

It seems obvious to us that escalating prices in Ireland in recent years must have placed home ownership beyond the reach of a considerable proportion of young – and not-so young – people. However, as mentioned earlier, some commentators, especially those closely aligned with the building industry or lending institutions invariably suggest that homes are as affordable as ever they were. The standard patter given on radio, television and in the newspapers goes something like this: There is really no problem! There should be no panic. It is certainly not a serious problem. The "fundamentals" of the Irish economy (never specified in any detail) are perfectly sound and people should not worry. The market forces of supply and demand, if left alone, will set things to right, will bring about "equilibrium" or balance in the market. All will be well – in due course!

Table 3.5   Is Irish Housing Over-Priced?

	Average New Prices (€)		Average 2nd hand Prices (€)	
	Whole Country	Dublin	Whole Country	Dublin
Actual 1994	72,732	81,993	69,877	82,772
Expected price in 2004 if increases as CPI	98,188	110,691	94,334	111,742
Expected price in 2004 if increases as Ave. Earnings	113,462	127,909	109,008	129,124
Expected price in 2004 if increases as Building Cost Index	117,826	132,829	113,200	134,091
Actual House Price 2004	249,191	322,628	294,667	389,791

Source: Based on *Housing Statistics Bulletin and Central Statistics Office*

Indeed the market is invariably seen as the answer to prayer, an automatic stabiliser. Of course existing tax incentives (a blatant interference in the beloved market) have been a boon to developers and should not be taken away at this stage by the government. To do so might cause a serious recession in the building industry and mass unemployment. Those who argue in these terms usually point to the number of homes constructed and purchased in recent years. Others use data from sources such as the *Household*

Budget Survey (HBS) to suggest that average expenditure on mortgages is quite low and as a proportion of total expenditure has remained low over several decades. Again, there is no problem. As an example, a recent book concluded that there was not an affordability problem on the basis of HBS data which showed that the average weekly mortgage payment in the year 1999/2000 was €74 (Fahey, Nolan and Maitre, 2004, p. 34). This manageable sum represented a mere 9.6 per cent of total household expenditure, a proportion which had declined from 10.4 per cent in 1994/95. On this basis, purchasing a home should scarcely present any serious difficulties even to the unemployed.

However, such a finding must seem remarkable to the general public and especially to those struggling to move out of the family home or rental accommodation. If such average mortgage repayments were reliable and representative, we would have no difficulty in also concluding that housing was quite affordable. However, as is often the case with social or economic statistics, in many respects, the average is not very helpful. In this specific case the average conceals the fact that a considerable number of mortgage holders have in fact quite modest loans taken out many years ago, while many more recent purchasers have large loans requiring substantial monthly payments. The low average of €74 would also include a considerable number of investors, second-home purchasers or speculators with ready cash and relatively low loan repayments. In this respect it is interesting to note that 58 per cent of loans paid in Dublin in 2003 were for no more than €200,000 (but average new house prices were far in excess of this). Indeed, 31 per cent of loans in Dublin in 2003 were actually for €150,000 or less (Department of the Environment, 2005). This suggests a considerable distortion of the average mortgage repayment figures due to a sizable proportion of house purchasers who can draw on independent resources (either their own or in the shape of once-off, tax-free "gifts" from parents) to reduce their levels of indebtedness. Less fortunate households will of course struggle to compete with such purchasers. In other words, the particular average figure for weekly mortgage repayments, which is influenced by an unknown number of longer-term loans or loans amounting to a small fraction of the real house price, disguises a great variety of social realities, and reveals little about the difficulties faced by many recent purchasers. Furthermore, the average is unhelpful in that it is a national figure, derived from a sample that encompasses enormous variation across cities, towns and countryside and different social classes, household compositions and age groups.

We should note a further problem with the average mortgage expenditure. This figure refers to the average housing costs incurred within a self-selecting or biased sample, made up of those households (in the main from higher income brackets) who have actually succeeded in acquiring a mortgage and purchasing a home – an achievement that presents considerable, even insurmountable, barriers to many households and is literally unimaginable to many people on low incomes or in vulnerable or marginalised positions. This raises the important question (at least from a social equality perspective) of housing *access*. In fact the biggest housing problems are those facing people excluded from accessing good housing at all because they lack the economic power to even participate, never mind compete in the house purchase market.

A clearer view of what is going on can be derived by examining the Household Budget figures across different income categories. In Figure 3.4, the entire population is grouped into four quartiles according to income, quartile 1 representing the poorest 25 per cent of households and quartile 4 the richest. It is then possible to examine the "social structure" of each tenure, as reflected in the relative dominance of upper, upper-middle, lower-middle and lower income groups. Those in home ownership (mortgaged) are overwhelmingly from the upper income or upper-middle income categories. In the main, people from lower income groups are excluded from this sector because they cannot afford to *access* home ownership at all – the cost of mortgage repayments are simply beyond them. The exact opposite prevails in local-authority housing, with over 52 percent of households in the lowest income quartile. The situation with regard to outright home ownership is also interesting in that 35 per cent of households are also in the lowest income quartile. Many of these are elderly households who may be described as "asset-rich, income-poor". The private rental sector, meanwhile, is strikingly close to the national situation. Just over 19 per cent of households in the sector are in the lowest income quartile, while almost 25 per cent are in the top quartile. Households in the middle quartiles make up almost 56 per cent of the sector. We return to this later, but the key issue here is that this sector is now housing households from a diverse range of income categories (and facing very different social predicaments) from the richest to the poorest households in the state (Duffy 2005).

Figure 3.4 Households in each Tenure by Income Quartile, 1999–2000

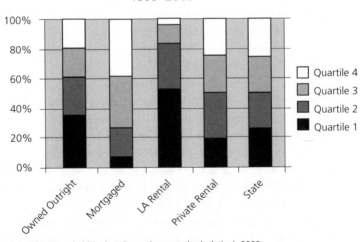

Source: CSO *Household Budget Survey* (requested calculation), 2002

There is of course a direct link between these different tenures. More households in higher income categories are now staying in private rental housing or in the family home due to the problems in *accessing* home ownership. This has the added effect of increasing rents in private rental accommodation as demand from higher-income households increases. Thus, the key question is not which sector is more unaffordable in relative terms – rather the interconnected problems across all tenures in the Irish housing system have generated a general crisis of access due to over-priced homes for purchase or for rent on the market and the limited development of social housing or other non-profit/non-market alternatives.

Finally, some more general concerns could be raised about the very concept of "affordability". The first, noted above, is the important distinction between affordability of access and the affordability of mortgage repayments for households already in home ownership. Redundancy or an increase in interest rates could well create considerable problems for those who have recently taken out mortgages.

A further important point relates to the definition of "affordability". Under Part V of the *Planning and Development Act* (2000a), an affordability threshold is defined. Basically, the premise is that a household should not have to spend more than 35 per cent of its annual income after deduction of income tax and PRSI (i.e. its disposable income) on mortgage repayments over the course of a year. This percentage is of course an arbitrary cut-off point, and it ignores the important question of inequality. A family in local authority housing may typically pay less than 10 per cent of their income on rent (due to the differential system), which means that this household would be defined as living in highly affordable accommodation – well below the 35 per cent threshold. Yet this might leave a very low *residual* income, such that the household is living in considerable income poverty and must struggle to meet even the most basic needs of everyday life – food, clothing, heating, costs associated with education, etc. By contrast, a household with a combined annual disposable income of €100,000 could conceivably have annual mortgage repayments of €36,000, that is 36 per cent of their disposable income. According to the above definition of affordability, their housing costs are now unaffordable. However, this leaves a more healthy residual income of €64,000. These definitional problems are well covered elsewhere (Hancock, 1993; Downey, 2003; O'Sullivan and Gibb, 2003; Redmond and Kernan, 2004) – we mention them at this point to highlight a further complexity of the affordability issue that has not been highlighted in the housing debate to date.

Given the inadequacies of arguments based on average weekly household expenditure on mortgages, how can we then arrive at a more useful picture of affordability problems which many households acutely experience? In fact a number of other affordability indicators or proxies give a clearer sense of the real situation than the average expenditure figures from the *Household Budget Survey*. Consider, for example, the ratio of average earnings to house prices. In 1984, the average price of a new home was €45,427, while the average industrial wage was €10,641, a ratio of 4.3 to 1. By 1994, the ratio had decreased slightly: average new house prices for the country as a whole (€72,732) were 4.2 times the size of the average industrial wage (€17,292). In Dublin, the ratio was 4.8. By June 2005, however, the ratio of house prices to average industrial earnings (€30,020) had deteriorated significantly to 9.1 to 1 for the country as a whole and 11.5 to 1 in Dublin (see also McNulty, 2003).

The situation in Dublin's "inner city" is even more problematic. In a detailed study of apartment prices, using a data base compiled at the Centre for Urban and Regional Studies in Trinity College, Kelly and MacLaran (2004) showed that two-bedroom units in November 2003 ranged between 10 and 18 times average industrial earnings. Three bed-room units completed in June 2003 were never less than 14 times average earnings and as high as 24 times in one particular instance. We give further details of this study in Tables 3.6 and 3.7

Table 3.6 Prices of Inner-city Residential Developments
Launched 1995-March 1996,
Expressed as Multipliers of Average Earnings (1995)

New prices 1995-6	Location	Launch Date	Av. Industrial Earnings			Av. Earnings Bank & Ins.		
			1 bed	2 bed	3 bed	1 bed	2 bed	3 bed
Bachelor's Walk	Dublin 1	May.95	2.43	4.68	5.49	1.93	3.72	4.36
Mountjoy Sq,	Dublin 1	Feb.96	2.63	3.35		2.13	2.71	
The Granary, Temple Bar	Dublin 2	Feb.95	5.49		11.55	4.36		9.17
Mellor Court, Liffey St. Lwr.	Dublin 2	June.95	2.73	3.90		2.18	3.11	
The Waterside, Ringsend	Dublin 4	Apr.95	2.56	3.93		2.04	3.13	
Charlotte Quay	Dublin 4	Jan.96	2.96	4.55		2.39	3.67	
Smithfield Village	Dublin 7	Mar.96	2.99	3.89	4.79	2.42	3.14	3.87
Temple Court, U. Dominick St.	Dublin 7	Feb.95	1.93			1.53		
The Maltings, Watling St.	Dublin 8	Nov.95	1.87	2.87		1.48	2.27	
Portobello Dock	Dublin 8	Feb.95	3.68	4.93		2.92	3.91	

Source: Kelly and MacLaran (2004)
Note: selected examples; see full table in Appendix

Table 3.7 Prices of Inner-city Residential Developments
Launched November 2003,
Expressed as Multipliers of Average Earnings

New prices	Location	Av. Industrial Earnings			Av. Earnings Bank & Ins.		
Nov. 2003		1 bed	2 bed	3 bed	1 bed	2 bed	3 bed
Spencer Dock	Dublin 1	10.78	12.13		8.69	9.78	
Liberty Corner, James Joyce St.	Dublin 1		12.47	16.85		10.05	13.58
Quartier Bloom, Ormond Quay	Dublin 2		18.37			14.81	
Gallery Quay, Gd Canal Dock	Dublin 2	9.61	14.16	15.33	7.74	11.41	12.36
Gasworks, Barrow St.	Dublin 4	10.45	13.48	18.87	8.42	10.87	15.21
Dock Mill, Barrow St.	Dublin 4	9.77	11.96	16.35	7.88	9.65	13.18
Smithfield Market	Dublin 7	12.13	14.49	17.69	9.78	11.68	14.26
Cork St, McGovern's Corner	Dublin 8		12.47	14.16		10.05	11.41
Portobello Wharf, Harold's Cross Bridge	Dublin 8			24.43			19.70

Source: Kelly and MacLaran (2004)
Note: Selected examples – full table in Appendix

A further indication of affordability can be gained from an examination of the incomes of borrowers. Table 3.8 shows that those with a combined income of less than €30,000 account for a decreasing proportion of total lending – from 9.9 per cent in 1998 to 2.2 per cent in 2004. Even borrowers with incomes up to €50,000 have fallen from 66.3 per cent to 26.1 per cent of the total during this period.

Table 3.8 Proportion of Borrowers for New Houses in Selected Income Ranges (combined incomes of borrowers)

	€30,000 or less	€30,001-50,000	€50,001 +
	%	%	%
1998	9.9	66.3	23.8
2004	2.2	26.1	71.7

Source: *Annual Housing Statistics Bulletin,* various editions

The typical borrowers have a combined income of more than €50,000, 37.7 per cent having between €50,000 and €70,000 and 34 per cent having incomes over €70,000.

In order to illustrate the challenge facing young aspiring home owners, let us take a typical young couple with two gross salaries of €30,000 each and disposable income after tax of €50,000, assuming a total deduction of €10,000. Our couple who have no children as yet wish to purchase a home in the Dublin area for €300,000, assuming, naively perhaps, that they can find such a home. They have managed to save or secure with the assistance of parents a deposit of 8 per cent i.e. €24,000. Since they are outside normal loan guide-lines acceptable to the lender, a helpful parent also agrees to act as guarantor on the loan. In the light of this, the lending agency is prepared to give them a mortgage of €276,000 at an APR of 3.6 per cent. Assuming a 20 year loan, their monthly repayments will be €5.83 per €1,000 borrowed i.e. €1,609 per month or €371 per week – 5 times the average figure from the *Household Budget Survey* cited earlier. This amounts to 38.6 per cent of their disposable income or 35.4 per cent after mortgage interest tax relief. However, there are other financial hurdles. On top of this, the couple will have to pay a further monthly payment on mortgage pro-tection in the event of the death of either party. The mini-mum payment expected on this is €30 per month. Solicitor's fees and other fees associated with conveyancing, would also arise. If the home had cost another €20,000 (i.e. €320,000) thereby bringing it above the threshold for stamp duty (€317,500), the couple would face an additional significant cost of about €12,000. If they manage to borrow this from another source, their payments would inevitably increase further. Is this home affordable? We believe that it simply is not! Even if the couple can avoid stamp duty, when the other additional payments are taken into account, this couple will be well above the already high so-called affordability limit of 35 per cent of after-tax income. If interest rates were to rise (triggering increased loan repayments), or if one of them becomes redundant or if future childcare costs have to be paid, the purchase may prove to be unsustainable. In an attempt to keep monthly payments to a manageable level, purchasers, with the agreement of the lending institutions, invariably resort to extending the term of the loan to 30 years or more and consequently settle down to a lifetime of mortgage repayments – a practice almost unheard of twenty years ago.

A further indicator of an affordability problem, particularly in the Dublin area where prices are highest, is illustrated by the growing extent of long-distance commuting. Due to the exceptional level of Dublin house prices illustrated earlier, large numbers of those working in the Dublin region who aspire to own a home at an affordable price have little option but to live within what estate agents loosely call "commuting distance of the capital". The Dublin commuting zones now include adjoining counties of Meath, Wicklow and Kildare, but also counties further afield such as Wexford, Carlow, Kilkenny, Tipperary, Portlaoise, Offaly, Westmeath, Longford, Cavan and Louth. As an illustration of this trend we might look at the rise in private house building in selected counties. For example, during 1994 a total of 2,500 private houses were built in the three counties adjoining Dublin – Meath, Kildare and Wicklow. This had increased to over 8,700 houses in 2004. In the more distant counties of Wexford, Westmeath and

Louth, almost 6,900 houses were built in 2004 compared to only 1,500 in 1994. Meanwhile, a range of national and provincial newspapers in recent years have carried advertisements on the joys of living in and commuting from such areas, often with the added advantage of generous tax incentives which we return to later in the book.

At first glance, the idea of leaving the city and moving to a remote village or town within commuting distance of work must seem attractive. The natural expectation for such people must be of a more leisurely pace, a small local school for the children, a new exciting opportunity to play a real part in a small local community and in general to achieve a better quality of life. All this is in contrast to the negative perceptions of city life, especially Dublin, with unaffordable house prices, daily traffic congestion with long delays, pressure on schools and generally a declining quality of life. Unfortunately, the comparison is not so simple and many of those moving to these outlying counties quickly get a rude awakening. Very few employment opportunities often exist in their new home areas and therefore the new arrivals must retain their jobs in the city. Furthermore, most of the counties listed above have limited public transport to the city. The result is that large numbers are now commuting each day by car.

Long-distance commuting brings with it a range of serious economic and social implications. One of the most obvious is the increased direct costs of petrol and wear and tear, often involving two cars. A further direct cost is the extra time spent in travelling, often in excess of two hours each way. This extra time is rarely taken into consideration by those building and selling homes in outlying counties but it is a very real cost and high for those involved. Apart from such "private" costs accruing to individuals, a huge "social" cost is imposed on other road users in terms of increased traffic congestion, increased fuel consumption, pollution and frustration. The reality for many commuters is that, in order to get to work on time, they must leave home well before 7 a.m. and rarely return before 8 p.m. Any aspiration to become "part of the community" or participate in community development in what was perceived to be an attractive rural village or town is unlikely to be realised.

Such experiences were widely reported by journalists who covered recent by-elections in the Dublin commuter belt of Meath and Kildare, and give a vivid picture of these new realities:

> Like others of my trade, I have spent some of the last few weeks travelling around the new housing estates of Meath and Kildare, soon to vote in byelections. Frankly, one can only despair.
>
> Faced with such an existence, and the prospect of four-hour daily commutes into Dublin, I would require vodka or Valium, or both, to get through the week.
>
> The estates have multiplied virus-like in recent years, and services are often non-existent.
>
> Yet we look on as if all of this has happened because of some law of nature that is not amenable to the hand of man. Such is not the case.
>
> Dublin's sprawl has been allowed to happen because of greed, a refusal to learn basic lessons from the past and, at times, what can only be described as stupidity of the highest order (Mark Hennessy, *Irish Times* March 5, 2005)

This article reported some of the experiences recorded in such commuter estates – leaving for work before 6 am, returning home after 10 pm, spending close to €2,000 a month on childcare, living in relatively poor quality housing. Such realities raise many social concerns:

> The lives that people are forced to lead in parts of Meath and Kildare because of this appalling administration, lack of foresight and hunger for Mammon are simply unbelievable.
>
> One crèche in Meath opens at 5.45 am to take its first

arrivals of the day from sleep-deprived parents, who then have to struggle to get into the capital.

Imagine such a day.

One stumbles out of bed at 5 am, or before, having probably had only a few hours' sleep, to get toddlers ready for a day in the care of others. Then drives on clogged-up roads to do a day's work, only to return home on equally gridlocked roads to begin the cycle once again.

Can anyone in their right minds believe that this is sustainable, that marriages and relationships will not sunder, that communities will not fail to grow, that children will be poorly brought up? Are we mad enough to believe that there will not be serious social consequences flowing from this, and soon (*ibid*)

Long-distance commuting is especially problematic for young couples with children. It is now commonplace for couples to leave children in a local creche, if available, from early morning until late evening. Alternatively, they must transport the children at an early hour to childcare facilities in or near their place of employment. If children are of school-going age, another challenge arises as population growth in such areas has invariably out-paced the provision of schools, recreational facilities and amenities. Until such schools and other facilities are provided (and this may take many years) parents must transport their children to schools in the city. Whichever option is chosen, the parents are denied access to, and enjoyment of, their children for long periods. The children are similarly without their parents during these periods. Without a doubt this situation represents a serious reduction in the quality of family life for all.

Such are the challenges and obstacles facing those who can manage to purchase their own homes, even at a considerable distance from employment opportunities. However, the most telling measure of affordability is the inability to purchase a home at all. As mentioned earlier, the officially accepted measure in recent years is a home whose loan repayments are no greater than 35 per cent of after-tax income (Government of Ireland, 2000a). Recent estimates carried out by the Local Authorities indicate that 33 per cent of new households over the period 2001-2006 would not be able to afford to purchase a home. This figure rises to 42 per cent in urban areas and is as high as 51 per cent in Fingal, 55 per cent in Dun Laoghaire Rathdown and 65 per cent in Waterford City (Local Authority Housing Strategies, 2001/2002 and Punch et al., 2002). Selected counties faced with the greatest affordability challenges (above the 33 per cent average) are listed in Table 3.9.

Table 3.9 Projected Housing Unaffordability,
New Households, 2001-2006

	% of new Households unable to afford home ownership
All	33
Urban areas	42
Counties above the national average:	
Cork	36
Donegal	50
Dublin City	36
DL/RD	55
Fingal	51
Longford	51
Monaghan	35
South Dublin	46
Waterford City	65
Wicklow	54

Source: Punch et al., 2002

THE CAUSES OF PRICE ESCALATION: DEMAND AND SUPPLY AGAIN

Clearly the significant rise in house prices over the past decade has caused a wide range of difficulties with serious social as well as economic implications. It is important therefore to isolate the main factors accounting for house price inflation. As we showed in Chapter 1, Ireland's housing system has changed from one where not-for-profit provision by the state, based on the need for homes, was significant to one in which the market, influenced by demand (implying ability to pay) has become the predominant influence on supply. Accordingly, let us briefly examine these factors of demand and supply. The significant growth of population over recent decades, coupled with increased employment opportunities and incomes have resulted in significant increases in the demand for housing (see, for example, the work of Bacon et al. 1998; Kenny, 1998; Roche, 2003; McQuinn, 2004; O'Sullivan, 2005). The growth of population has been particularly strong in the Dublin region and in the adjoining Mid-East comprising the counties of Wicklow, Meath and Kildare (see Appendix Table A3). Between them, these two regions increased in population by almost 630,000 over the last 40 years. At the same time, the supply of housing has been inadequate to meet this dramatic increase in demand. When supply of housing on the market is inadequate to meet demand, an increase in prices inevitably results, leaving developers in a strong position to charge "what the market will bear". In this situation the buyer has little or no bargaining power and within a short space of time the price of a further block of housing can even increase significantly, despite no increase in cost to the developer. This is, in effect, what has happened over the last decade – the market has failed to supply sufficient housing to meet demand and to stabilise prices. From a consumer viewpoint, this is a fundamental flaw in the market mechanism.

Apart from the increase in population and incomes mentioned above, demand has also been influenced by a number of other factors, in particular, low interest rates over an extended period and the ready willingness of the lending institutions to make significant funding available to borrowers (Fitzpatrick & McQuinn, 2004). Much of this lending has invariably been in breach of Central Bank guidelines, and has encouraged large-scale borrowing. In order to protect the interest of their shareholders, the lending institutions invariably seek guarantees from parents or others as well as retaining the deeds of homes. Such flexible lending policies obviously push up demand and contribute significantly to house price increases. It has also resulted in a dramatic increase in housing indebtedness on the part of the Irish. Over the five year period 1999-2003 alone over €57 billion in housing loans were approved by banks and building societies, the banks responsible for about three quarters of this sum. One respected Central Bank economist has argued that this significant growth in mortgage lending could, if interest rates or unemployment increases, put many households well above any acceptable affordability ratio. There is also evidence that the "relaxed lending" environment is likely to lead to a higher rate of mortgage arrears among households (Kearns, 2003).

Second, lending institutions have been prepared to give substantial loans for investment in housing to considerable numbers of people who view housing as an investment or speculative opportunity, even on a short-term basis, due partly to the stock market slump in recent years and a move away from investment in equities to property. Such investment or speculative activity is inevitably encouraged by the rapid and uncontrolled escalation in prices illustrated earlier and, further, by the reduction in capital-gains tax to a mere 20 per cent in 1997. This trend is reflected in the increase over the years in the proportion of borrowers purchasing homes who were already home owners rather than first time buyers as shown by Table 3.10. This Table only contains information on those who purchased new second homes with a mortgage and given that a considerable number of large-scale investors in housing have access to sufficient capital not to require a mortgage at all (see Appendix A2), it undoubtedly underestimates the extent of house purchase for investment or speculative purposes. This has placed further upward pressure on house prices and has resulted in a significant displacement of aspiring first-time buyers in recent years. In a short period between 2001 and 2004, Table 3.10 shows that the proportion of first-time buyers has fallen from 63 per cent to 48 per cent for the country as a whole, with an even greater fall in the Dublin area (Department of Environment, Heritage and Local Government, 2005). In contrast, an increasing number of purchasers are buying a second residential property while, in exceptional cases, buyers purchase entire blocks of houses or apartments. The percentage in the "other" category, which comprises mainly investors and holiday home owners, increased from 37 per cent to 52 per cent for the country as a whole. Over the last decade, such buyers could purchase for speculative purposes on the assumption of accruing large capital gains, modest capital gains tax payments, high rents and little regulation during the period the property was held. Furthermore, more

Table 3.10 Ownership Status of New House Buyers and Others (%)

	Whole Country		Dublin	
	First-Time Buyers	Others	First-Time Buyers	Others
2001	63.0	37.0	65.8	34.2
2004	48.4	51.6	47.7	52.3

Source: *Annual Housing Statistics Bulletin*, 2004

than 104,000 dwellings bought for investment purposes and 39,000 holiday homes, many with tax incentives, lie vacant in all parts of the country at a time of apparent national housing need. There seems little doubt that tax-driven demand by investors, in particular, has contributed significantly to this and to the increase in house prices (Fitzgerald, 2005). We return to this issue in Chapter 4.

THE ROLE OF GOVERNMENT POLICIES

Government policies have, over many years, shown a heavy bias towards market provision of housing and to home owners thus contributing to the escalation in house prices. The various incentives have been as follows:

- Remission of rates on new housing prior to 1978. Residential rates abolished since 1978
- A residential property tax introduced in 1984. Abolished in 1997
- No capital gains tax on sale of principal residence
- Capital gains tax reduced on second homes from 40% to 20% in 1997
- No stamp duty for first time buyers on new housing for owner occupation
- No stamp duty on second hand house for first time buyers up to certain size
- Mortgage interest tax relief.
- Cash grant to first-time buyers over many years. Abolished 2004.
- Significant discounts to Local Authority tenants to encourage owner occupation. Very favourable terms on Local Authority mortgages.
- Surrender grant offered in the 1980s to encourage Local Authority tenants to move out of public housing and purchase in the private market

- Shared ownership and affordable housing schemes designed to encourage owner occupation with public assistance.

Mortgage interest tax relief, the abolition of residential rates since the late 1970s, stamp duty remission and first-time buyer grants were presumably intended to reduce the cost of housing for owner-occupiers and as such they proved popular political initiatives. In reality, however, with very few alternatives to house purchase, they ultimately contributed to increasing demand for market-driven housing and thus to higher house prices, creating an affordability problem even for relatively well-off purchasers (O'Connell and Quinn, 1999).

Furthermore, housing produced for sale on the market has also long enjoyed very generous tax treatment relating to capital gains. There is no capital gains tax on the main residence, and the reduction in this tax to 20 per cent in the November 1997 Budget for second or investment homes exacerbated the situation in relation to house prices while also encouraging a view of housing as an investment and a vehicle for wealth creation.

A residential property tax introduced in 1984 was also recommended by the Commission on Taxation and with considerable justification since there was, in effect, virtually no taxation on wealth in Ireland and the country was thus out of line with a whole range of other European countries (Commission on Taxation, 1985; Callan, 1991). The property tax was set at 1.5 per cent of any increase in the estimated value of a home over a certain threshold in a particular year. It applied to people on relatively high incomes in substantial properties and affected only a relatively small section of the overall population. However, on the assumption that the tax would eventually be imposed on the wider population, it was unpopular with the general public and especially so with those who owned substantial homes. It could certainly be fairly argued that the tax discriminated against a high proportion of Dublin residents whose homes were arguably more valuable than those in other parts of the country. In any case, a concerted campaign was mounted by high profile public figures and those with significant property interests to get rid of the tax altogether rather than attempt to rectify its shortcomings. The residential property tax was thus abolished by the government in 1997. It is significant that house prices remained very stable or increased at a moderate rate during most of the period since the introduction of the Residential Property Tax in 1984 and up to 1995. After its abolition in 1997, house prices virtually took off, soaring by 23 per cent for the country as a whole and by 32 per cent in Dublin in the year 1997/98. While the property tax was obviously not the only factor influencing house prices, we believe that its retention would have dampened down demand and price inflation to the benefit of house purchasers.

HOUSING SUPPLY: LAND, PLANNING AND SERVICES

Let us now turn to the main factors influencing the supply of housing. If supply were adequate to meet demand in the market system, house prices would settle or as the jargon puts it, there would be "equilibrium" or balance between demand and supply. In response to the dramatic increase in demand, fueled by the various factors mentioned above, the supply of housing units by private developers and housebuilders has, in fact, increased significantly from about 30,000 units in the early 1990s to almost 72,000 in 2004. This was an impressive performance. However, as shown earlier there has been little sign of prices stabilising. It seems obvious therefore that the market is failing to deliver due to the inflated demand (caused particularly by investors and speculators availing of tax incentives and second home owners) as well as problems on the supply side.

What are these supply-side problems? One factor of central importance is the supply and availability, as well as the price, of land suitable for housing (see, for example, McNulty, 2003; Roche, 2003). The supply of land suitable for housing is relatively fixed, although there is regular pressure from some developers, especially in the main urban centres, to increase the supply by building on wetlands or floodplains (often with serious flooding implications), purchasing amenity land or sites of scientific interest in the hope of obtaining planning permission and less often by reclamation from the sea. With a relatively fixed supply and excess demand, even for land zoned for agricultural or amenity purposes and without planning permission, it is inevitable that there will be an upward pressure on land prices. When land is rezoned for housing and planning permission thus seems possible, the price of land will rise further. In relation to land prices, the Irish Home Builders Association estimated that average site prices in Dublin had risen by 200 per cent between 1995 and 1998, accounting for 36 per cent of the average house price in 1998 compared to 21 per cent in 1995. Recent land sales indicate that the proportion taken up by the price of land could be as high as 40-50 per cent (Casey, 2003). These exceptional increases in the price of land are invariably passed on to house purchasers in the form of higher house prices. While it seems obvious to us that the supply and price of land are critical determinants of house prices, some commentators argue that land prices have little to do with the increase in house prices. Rather, they suggest that it is the other way around – the prices developers expect to procure from house sales will dictate what they are prepared to pay for land. This so-called "residual" theory of land prices is not of course unreasonable. If developers expected to procure modest prices for houses, they would be unlikely to pay high prices for the land on which the building is constructed. However, in an amazing sleight of hand, the cost of land is therefore dismissed as being irrelevant to dealing with house prices and affordability problems. The price of housing could of course be a factor influencing the price of land, but that does not mean that land is an irrelevant factor or that its availability and price themselves do not play a central role in influencing and determining house prices. As Evans puts it:

> We cannot ... draw the illegitimate conclusion that the supply of land or the planned allocation of land to different uses does not matter and has no effect on the price of land and the price of housing   (Evans, 2004. pp. 18-19)

This surely is common sense. Land is scarce in the Dublin area. Therefore, it sells at very high prices, if only due to "hope value" i.e. the possibility that its price will rise in the future. This cost factor inevitably feeds into high house prices. In other parts of the country, especially in rural areas, land is not so scarce. Therefore, land prices are much lower than in the Dublin area with resultant lower house prices.

Those who argue that land prices have no role in the escalation of house prices invariably want little or no intervention in relation to land. Nothing much has changed. Over thirty years ago, Justice Kenny's Committee made various proposals for policy change in order to deal with the high cost of land and the related problem of "betterment". The Committee recommended that the High Court should be given power to designate areas where land would be required for housing or other purposes. The local authorities would have power to acquire such land at existing use value plus 25 per cent. At the time, the recommendations of the Kenny Report (1973) were ignored on the dubious grounds that these were unconstitutional – which they were not – and this "decision" to do nothing played its part in subsequent massive rezoning windfalls to landowners, developers and speculators.

There is evidence to suggest that land suitable for housing in some parts of the country and especially in the Dublin area is controlled by a relatively small number of landowners and developers. With various constraints affecting supply in the short term (e.g. lack of services such as water, sewage, roads and other facilities), a relatively small number of developers-speculators can purchase and hoard land and release it slowly, thereby exercising a degree of control over prices and profits from housing. It has been shown that over recent years about twenty five major developers (many of them companies) have gained control over 50 per cent of land suitable for housing in the Fingal county in the Dublin region (Casey, 2003). This small group can effectively operate a monopoly-type influence on the availability and price of land and, as a result, the price of housing. The significant difference illustrated earlier between building costs and the price of housing suggests that there are indeed some additional and exceptional elements in the final house price. Land is undoubtedly one of these.

Any monopoly-type activity represents a diminution of competition and a serious inefficiency in the system. On these grounds alone, this matter deserves urgent attention. Of even greater concern is the part the Local Authorities play, sometimes too readily, but often under duress, in further enriching such landowners when, every five years or more often in some cases, in the interests of the common good, they re-zone agricultural land for residential purposes – a further critical factor affecting supply. The price of such land can multiply a hundred–fold overnight even though the owners have carried out no productive activity whatsoever. The final irony is that, having rezoned the land to facilitate an increase in the supply of housing in the interest of the common good, the Local Authority becomes ultimately responsible for the provision of services, such as roads, water and sewage, although some of this cost may be recouped from the developer.

THE GOVERNMENT AND LOCAL AUTHORITY RESPONSE

The difficulties associated with purchasing a home are not of course new. They became obvious from the mid 1990s and in 1998 the Government commissioned Peter Bacon and Associates to analyse the problem and suggest solutions. While Bacon produced three useful reports, it must be noted that they were all almost exclusively concerned with the problem of house prices and paid no serious attention to the other tenures despite the critical links between them. Furthermore, the underlying philosophy pervading all three reports was that the market remains the most useful mechanism for the provision of housing. The problems of those who were unable to contemplate home ownership and were by extension in need of social housing received virtually no attention (Bacon and Associates, 1998, 1999, 2000).

The Bacon proposals to the government included :

- An increase in the supply of private housing
- A serviced land initiative – the lack of serviced land was seen as a constraint on the supply of housing
- A faster turnover in planning permissions – delays in getting permission was also seen as a problem
- The elimination of mortgage interest tax relief to those purchasing second homes – investors were seen to be competing unfairly with first-time buyers
- The introduction of a speculative tax to deter speculators

In response, the government since 1998 has placed a great emphasis on increasing the supply of private housing (Government of Ireland, 1999a). It also accepted the need to move more rapidly on the provision of serviced land for housing and agreed to increase the number of planning graduates with a view to reducing delays with planning permission. As regards Bacon's proposal that mortgage interest relief should be eliminated for investors, this was indeed implemented for a short period, but under pressure from property interests the then Minister for Finance, Mr. McCreevy, re-instated this incentive. Meanwhile, the proposed anti-speculative tax was never introduced.

In 1999, the government introduced an Affordable Housing Scheme similar to one previously adopted in 1997 by Dublin Docklands Development Authority. These schemes were designed to provide housing for sale at a discount below the prices which could be obtained on the market to those below a certain income threshold. Two further Affordable Housing schemes were introduced, one in the 2000 Planning Act and one in the *Sustaining Progress* agreement in 2002. The 2000 Planning Act also introduced the concept of a Special Development Zone, the first of these which was subsequently designated at Adamstown in the Dublin region with the intention of "fast-tracking" the supply of housing. As a result of the same Act, the planning authorities produced a range of housing strategies over the period 2001-02 in which they proposed major rezoning of land for housing. During the five year period 1999 to 2003 a total of 2,800 affordable homes were completed and a further 4,800 were in progress (Department of the Environment, Heritage and Local Government, 2003).

As part of the *Sustaining Progress* agreement in 2002, the government also committed itself to providing an extra 10,000 affordable houses over the period to 2006. In view of the slow progress with this proposal, the Government announced in August 2005 the establishment of an "Affordable Homes Partnership", chaired by Mr. Des Geraghty, in order to bring forward land and to speed up the provision of affordable housing.

CONCLUSION

This chapter clearly establishes that purchasing a home has become a major challenge for many individuals and couples, even those in relatively well-paid employment. For many more it is an impossible dream given that house prices have been completely out of line with other indices for more than a decade. We cannot see any justification for a continuation of this situation. It is important to stress that the level of house price increases could have the overall effect of slowing down or seriously compromising the considerable economic progress achieved in Ireland over the last decade. There is the questionable argument that existing home owners have "gained" significantly from price increases. While some may argue that there are benefits from a housing "wealth effect", whether real or imaginary, one serious downside is the increasing tendency of households, using homes as security, to take out substantial, and arguably unsustainable, loans for personal consumption. Furthermore, those who have struggled to purchase homes in recent times have taken on large and often excessive loans. If interest rates were to rise, the level of indebtedness could become unsustainable for many. Indeed, we would question whether the current level of mortgage debt is justified in the light of many other urgent requirements in the Irish economy.

Notes
1. If we are correct that Irish house prices are over-valued, this suggests that Ireland's income as measured by Gross National Product is similarly inflated since final house prices are a significant element in this.

Chapter 4

The Rental Market: A Real Alternative?

The private rented sector has had a chequered history in Ireland. Once a predominant form of accommodation, it has suffered from a generally negative image due to a perception of high rents, poor standards and insecurity of tenure. It has also been labelled "the forgotten sector" due to the relative disinterest of the state in dealing with these various problems (O'Brien and Dillon, 1982). As a result, private renting has long been regarded by many as a short-term option before either purchasing a home or renting a less expensive one with greater security from a Local Authority. Despite the sector's negative image, we must emphasise that there are many landlords who have provided and continue to offer first class accommodation at reasonable rents and who offer secure homes for long periods to satisfied tenants. Furthermore, this sector can play a most important role in any housing system by providing accommodation for those who are either unwilling or unable to purchase and who cannot gain access to Local Authority housing. The sector can offer a valuable and flexible option for a whole range of income groups and particularly for workers on relatively short employment contracts and for students attending third level institutions. In recent years, it has also arguably fulfilled a useful role in providing accommodation for low-income groups eligible for rent supplement under the government's Supplementary Welfare Scheme.

OVERVIEW OF PRIVATE RENTING IN IRELAND

The current structure of the private rented sector in Ireland is set out in Table 4.1. Now a total of 141,500 units, it had declined persistently for many years. For example, in 1961 there were 116,000 units; this had declined to 81,000 by 1991. However, it had shown a remarkable increase of 60,000 units or 74 per cent by 2002. The vast majority of the units (115,600 units) are now furnished, with most still in detached, semi-detached or terraced housing. Almost 43 per cent of the accommodation is now in flats/apartments and in the light of recent construction patterns, especially in the main urban centres, this is likely to be a more important element in the years ahead. The private rented sector accommodates a total of 343,000 people, two thirds living in traditional housing and the remainder in flats/apartments. See Table 4.2. The largest concentration of private rented accommodation is in the Dublin area (38.8 per cent), followed by Cork, Galway and Limerick. See Table 4.3. A total of 60,500 units were built since 1980 while slightly more (62,000) were built prior to that date. Almost 44,000 units pre-date 1960. See Table 4.4.

The private rental sector presents a microcosm of the uneven realities in housing and in Irish society more generally. At one end, private renting is typified by high-grade accommodation occupied in the main by high-income households from upper-middle class or élite groups (such as visiting delegates from multi-national corporations). The mid-part of the sector is largely occupied by middle-class, salaried workers, who also have considerable social-class advantages, as reflected in job opportunities and educational achievement. These include a considerable (and in recent years rapidly increasing) proportion of younger households who have had to postpone becoming homeowners due to the affordability problems created by house-price escalation over recent years.

Table 4.1 Accommodation Type in the Private Rented Sector, 2002

	Furnished	Unfurnished	Total
Detached house	17,273	7,021	24,294
Semi-detached house	27,000	6,357	33,357
Terraced house	17,255	4,885	22,140
Flat in purpose built block	29,526	4,118	33,644
Flat in conventional house	19,172	2,488	21,660
Flat in commercial building	4,406	662	5,068
Other	944	352	1,296
TOTAL	115,576	25,883	141,459

Source: *Census of Population*, 2002

Table 4.2 Number of Persons in Private Rented Accommodation by Type, 2002

	Furnished	Unfurnished	Total
Detached house	48,950	21,208	70,158
Semi-detached house	79,890	18,804	98,694
Terraced house	45,513	12,287	57,800
Flat in purpose built block	60,324	7,428	67,752
Flat in conventional house	31,754	4,061	35,815
Flat in commercial building	8,376	1,267	9,643
Other	2,399	815	3,214
TOTAL	277,206	65,870	343,076

Source: *Census of Population*, 2002

Table 4.3 Main Location of Private Rented Accommodation, 2002

	Number of Units	% of Total
Dublin	54,831	38.8
Cork	17,389	12.3
Limerick	6,729	4.8
Galway	9,107	6.4
All other areas	53,403	37.7
Total	141,459	100.0

Source: *Census of Population,* 2002

Table 4.4 Accommodation in the Private Rented Sector by Year Built

	Pre-1960	1961-1970	1971-1980	1981-1990	1991-1995	1996 -	Un-known	Total
Un-furnished	9.923	1,681	2,457	2,451	2,156	4,937	2,278	25,883
Furnished	33,862	5,353	8,727	11,174	12,877	26,899	16,684	115,576
Total	43,785	7,034	11,184	13,625	15,033	31,836	18,962	141,459

Source: *Census of Population,* 2002

At the lower end, a different set of realities prevails, as low-income and disadvantaged households with limited job opportunities face low-paid work, unemployment or outright marginalisation and problems of insecurity and relatively high rents for low-quality dwellings. Economic hardship can also translate rent hikes into a personal housing crisis and potential homelessness. This dual reality can be seen in the range of incomes of private rental tenants. As noted earlier, the most recent *Household Budget Survey* revealed that just over 19 per cent of households in the sector are in the lowest income quartile, while almost 25 per cent are in the top quartile. Households in the middle quartiles make up almost 56 per cent of the sector.

Further evidence on the social structure of the private-rental sector can be derived by examining the economic status of households in each quartile (see also Punch, 2005). This is set out in Table 4.5, which provides better insight as to the variable social predicament facing households with differential incomes within the private rental sector. The 19 per cent of households renting in the market who fall into the lowest income quartile are in the main economically inactive (retired or otherwise marginal to the labour force). Just over a quarter are unemployed, while just over 15 per cent are at work (low-wage workers). By contrast, a considerable majority (86.5 per cent) of private rental households falling in the upper income quartile are dual earners. The above shows that while one cohort of households relying on the private rental sector for housing are either low-paid workers, unemployed, elderly or otherwise marginalised, others are economically advantaged, being on high incomes and in many cases possessing dual sources of income.

Table 4.5. Private rental households by income quartile and economic status (%)

		Quartile 1	Quartile 2	Quartile 3	Quartile 4	State
At work	One person	15.0	59.1	38.3	9.4	34.7
	One or more	0.7	12.7	52.6	86.5	35.8
Unemployed		25.1	6.8	0.4	0.0	4.2
Economically inactive	Pension	18.7	3.5	0.0	0.0	14.9
	Other	40.5	17.9	8.7	4.1	10.5
Total		100.0	100.0	100.0	100.0	100.0

Source: CSO *Household Budget Survey* (requested calculation), 2002

The well-documented difficulties facing first-time buyers in the context of escalating house and land prices also have inter-tenure effects, with important ramifications for low-income renters. The access problems in the private owner-ship sector arising from price escalation have meant that middle-class households have increasingly had to postpone purchasing, many of them becoming long-term renters instead. This has created extra pressure at the upper- and mid-points of the rental market. One important result is what has been well described as a "crowding-out" effect, as the transfer of housing demand from home ownership to private renting has led to diminishing accessibility for dis-advantaged households (Downey, 1998, 2003). This tenden-cy is also reflected in income trends within the private rental sector. See Figure 4.1. In the mid 1990s, tenants were predominantly from the lowest income quartile (over 31 per cent), while less than 19 per cent were from the upper quartile. By the end of the decade, most tenants were from the two highest income quartiles, including over 24 per cent in the highest.

Figure 4.1. Income Distribution in the Private rented Sector Private rented households by income quartile, 1994-95 and 1999-2000

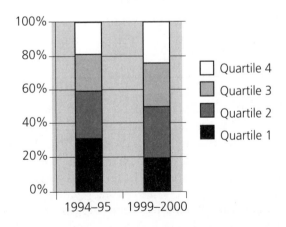

Source: CSO *Household Budget Survey,* various editions

Consequently, there is also a growing concern with housing access and affordability in the private rental sector, with most important implications for poorer households. The problem must be understood as an inter-tenural issue, as the high price of private ownership as illustrated in Chapter 3 drives demand upwards in the private rental sector, while the low levels of provision and restricted access typical of public housing in Ireland (to be examined in Chapter 4) further restricts mobility and options for many people.

The boom in house prices has created an incentive for landlords in possession of houses in multiple occupancy, to realise the capital value of their asset by de-tenanting, converting and selling the property into owner occupancy. Traditionally multiple occupancy was the only affordable option for poorer households. The process at work is essentially one of "gentrification", as historic patterns of disinvestment in low-grade properties (rented out for many years as cheap but poor quality residential units) are reversed and the considerable "rent gap" (the gap between historic and potential ground rents) is exploited by upgrading the use (flats become apartments) or converting and selling for ownership. Further pressures derive from the accumulation imperative, which demands that any residential investment produce a satisfactory rental yield above the cost of servicing the mortgage. As a result, rental levels have generally tracked the boom in house prices, generating windfalls for those in a position to exploit the enhanced exchange-value potential in a tight market and at the same time contributing to a real housing crisis for poorer households. Finally, a further unintended source of pressure on the traditional cheaper options is the implementation of (necessary but basic) regulations for minimum standards, which also have the unfortunate potential side effect of reducing the only accessible and affordable accommodation open to poorer households in the market.

Many people on lower incomes simply cannot afford to pay for accommodation which conforms to minimum standards.

HIGH RENTS AND RENT REGULATION: THE CONTINUING DEBATE

One of the most pressing and persistent problems in the private rental sector, at least from the tenant viewpoint, has been the high level of rents and the uncertainty regarding future rent increases. Attempts to control or regulate rents have always met with opposition from landlord interests, while being applauded by tenants. Most economists have tended to argue that any form of rent regulation will tend to put pressure on landlords who either neglect their rented properties or possibly dispose of them, thus reducing the supply of accommodation. One well-known economist, Assar Lindbeck, even argued, without much evidence, that rent regulation had worse consequences for cities than the hydrogen bomb! (Quoted in Parkin et al. 2003). However, recent research suggests that it is not quite as simple as that. Therefore, it is worth looking more closely at the vexed question of rent control. Is there a case for this form of regulation, or is it a policy without a future that serves only to constrict the availability of accommodation? This issue has been a topic of debate for many years. Those who favour regulation argue that the market for rental accommodation is generally "imperfect", characterized by poor information about availability of accommodation, excess demand for limited accommodation and consequently "monopoly-type" power in the hands of landlords. Competition is often insufficient to drive rents down, and supply responds slowly and unevenly to demand in many circumstances. There is also the further argument that housing, like education and health, is a social necessity and thus must be regulated in the interests of equity and social justice. On the other hand, those who oppose regulation believe (misguidedly in our view) that the market for rental accommodation is perfectly competitive and that no intervention is required, either for efficiency or equity reasons.

Controls on rents were introduced in several countries in Europe from the First World War and remained for many years. Rent controls were similarly introduced in the United States just after the start of the Second World War. These early rent control programmes are often termed "hard" or "first generation" controls. They tended to be harsh from a landlord's viewpoint, in that rents were frozen for a period. This form of control was particularly unpopular among most economists who argued that rent controls discouraged new construction, deferred maintenance of property, created black markets and resulted in a reduction in private rental accommodation. Few would argue with the contention that these "first generation" controls were problematic and unhelpful in the long term.

Since the 1970s, however, the rent control debate has altered significantly and it is now widely accepted, even among economists, that a well-designed rent control programme can in fact be beneficial (Arnott, 1995). Re-introduced in many European countries and North America, this new "soft" rent control or, more accurately rent regulation, has been termed "second generation". This newer approach to regulation permitted rent increases related to the rate of inflation and improvements to the property, as well as assuring landlords a "reasonable" rate of return. Provision was also often made for decontrol. Such rent regulation has often been accompanied by provisions to improve security of tenure and to provide appeal procedures regarding rents and evictions. Clearly, the concept of second generation rent regulation is very different from first generation rent freezes. Despite arguments regarding the dire consequences of rent regulation, there is no empirical evidence to suggest such negative effects accompanied regulation in a European context, and the effects in North America have been "almost imperceptible" (Arnott, 1995).

Why then has there been such opposition, at least in some quarters, to rent regulation? In our view, the objections are largely ideological. Those who oppose rent regulation believe in the free, perfectly competitive market; those who advocate rent regulation do not. Those opposing rent regulation also invariably oppose the concept of a minimum wage, arguing that this would result in increased unemployment. In fact, the introduction of a minimum wage in Ireland coincided with a dramatic reduction in unemployment. At the very least, rent regulation can be justified when an imperfect market exists, and this is invariably the case in relation to housing.

Irrespective of the form of rent control, the decline in private rented accommodation over many decades was inevitable in view of the consistent move to owner occupation, the insecurity which usually accompanied private renting, relatively poor standards of accommodation provided to tenants and the uncertainty regarding future rents. In the major urban centres such as Dublin, slum clearance and re-development programmes from early in the century also eliminated a considerable number of privately rented properties.

A rigid form of first generation rent control was introduced in Ireland in the Increase in Rent and Mortgage (War Restrictions) Act, 1915, in order to protect tenants from exploitation during the First World War. It had a negative impact on landlords who owned such dwellings. The Act provided that rents must be restricted to the "standard rent" at which a dwelling was let in August 1914 and increases were limited to a proportion of rate or property tax increases or the costs of structural improvements carried out by the landlord. The landlord was also restricted in recovering possession of the dwelling, conferring, in effect, security of tenure on the tenant. The legislation was only intended to remain in force for the War period, but it was in fact continued in a long series of temporary Acts up to 1960. The Rent Restrictions Act, 1960, repealed all previous legislation and further amendments were made in the Rent Restrictions Act, 1967, and in further acts subsequently up to 1981. While the new legislation provided rent control over mainly unfurnished dwellings in the private rented sector an entire range of dwellings were in fact de-controlled e.g. houses or flats constructed after 1941 and buildings reconstructed into separate and self-contained flats after 1960. The end result was that by the early 1970s there were no more than 50,000 dwellings in Ireland subject to first generation rent control (NESC, 1976; O'Brien and Dillon, 1982).

While the Rent Restrictions Acts gave considerable protection to particular tenants it can be argued that it imposed an undue burden on landlords who were arguably chosen arbitrarily to accept an uneconomic rent without compensation. Even philanthropic housing providers, such as the Iveagh Trust, attributed its financial difficulties to the rigid form of rent control imposed by the Rent Restrictions Acts (Aalen, 1990). In a Supreme Court judgement (*Blake v Attorney General* [1982] IR, 117), it was held that Parts II and IV of the 1960 Act, which dealt with the rents of controlled dwellings and the landlord's right to recover possession, constituted an unjust attack on property rights, guaranteed by Article 40.3.2 of the Irish Constitution. The main basis of the judgement was that the previous legislation was arbitrary in that it did not apply to all landlords. Secondly, there were no provisions to review rents or to compensate landlords for losses or improvements. This led to the passing of the Housing (Private Rented Dwellings) Act 1982 and an amending Act in 1983 which gave formerly rent-controlled tenants some security of tenure (subject to various exclusions) and in the absence of agreement between landlord and tenant, allowed rents to be determined by a Rent Tribunal (Coughlan, 1998, pp. 345-348). The rent, if determined by the Tribunal, was to be a just and proper rent having regard to the nature, character and location of the dwelling, the terms of the tenancy, the means of landlord and tenant, the date and purchase price paid, the length of occupancy, and the numbers in the dwelling. Once the terms of the tenancy had been fixed by the Tribunal, they would remain in force for a period of four years and nine months unless the landlord made improvements to the dwelling. In other words, rent would be regulated in a fair and reasonable manner from the viewpoint of both landlord and tenant. This latter approach might be termed "second generation" rent control/regulation as opposed to the previous more rigid "first generation" approach. Situations where rent is regulated in this way have however been a declining feature of the private rental sector in Ireland and it was estimated that by 1987 less than 11,000 dwellings were subject to rent control (Commission on Private Rented Residential Sector, 2000, p.10).

The fact that the Irish Supreme Court ruled that the 1960 Act and subsequent legislation relating to "first generation" rent control was unconstitutional does not of course mean that a similar judgement would be reached in all cases and at all times in regard to rent regulation. A property right can in fact be circumscribed by the state if (i) the means chosen is rationally connected to the objective and not arbitrary, unfair or based on irrational considerations; (ii) if it impairs the right as little as possible and (iii) if the effect on rights is proportional to the objective. It is also important to note that Article 43.2.1 of the Constitution states that private property rights "ought to be regulated by the principles of social justice", while 43.2.2 proclaims that the State may delimit by law the exercise of such rights in the interests of the "common good". This was also the conclusion in a range of legal judgements. See, for example,

Heaney v Ireland [1994], 3, IR, 593, *Dieler v the Irish Land Commission* [1984] and All Party Oireachtas Committee on the Constitution (2004) for a full review of cases.

It is also worth noting that the Constitution Review Group reporting in 1996 argued as follows:

> "If the state is to function, property rights must yield to a wide variety of countervailing interests, among them the redistribution of wealth, the protection of the environment, and the necessity for consumer protection. This in turn means that the state must have extensive taxation powers, powers of compulsory acquisition and a general capacity to regulate (and even in some cases extinguish) property rights" (Constitution Review Group. 1996).

INSECURITY, HIGH RENTS AND POOR STANDARDS: SOME EVIDENCE

Over 20 years ago, a detailed study on behalf of Threshold (the housing advice and advocacy organisation) was carried out by O'Brien and Dillon (1982). At that time, they identified a number of fundamental difficulties facing tenants in the private rental sector. In particular, they identified what they termed "the almost non-existent security of tenure afforded to the tenant" and the ease of eviction. In the absence of a lease or written agreement, the landlord could take action for possession irrespective of whether or not a breach of agreement or default took place (O'Brien and Dillon, p. 18). Most tenancies could be terminated with 28 days notice at the whim of the landlord (i.e. there was no requirement to justify the eviction or even to inform the tenant of the grounds for eviction – what is often termed a "no-fault notice to quit"). Eviction (actual or threatened) was the single most common difficulty identified in the Threshold survey of 3,000 households over a two-year

period (1978-1980), a problem experienced by 972 households or 32.4% of the total (O'Brien and Dillon, p. 40). The
next most frequently reported concern related to rental
increases (18.8%). A further difficulty emphasised in the
study (669 cases) was the high level of rents in relation to
average costs in other housing tenures and the ability of the
landlord to increase rents at frequent intervals. According
to the authors, rents were increasing "at an alarming rate"
in the years 1981 and 1982 – the average increase being
sought was 34.5 per cent (O'Brien and Dillon, p. 52). Two
decades later, matters were little better. Over the period
1998-2001, average rents in Dublin increased by 53 per cent
– far in excess of the consumer price index. It now seems
that rental increases in recent years have tracked house
price increases, leading to a crisis of rented affordability.[1] A
further comparative study by the European Central Bank
showed that the highest level of rent increases over the
1997-2001 period across the European Union was recorded
in Ireland (European Central Bank, 2003). Rents apparently fell over the period 2002 to 2004 but increased again from
2005. In any case, in 2005 rents were 30 to 40 per cent higher than they had been seven years earlier – well above normal inflationary tendencies over this period (Gunne, 2004;
DAFT, 2005). This is a serious concern, particularly as a
viable rental option is likely to become increasingly important both socially and economically as greater levels of vulnerability and flexibility are introduced to labour markets
through increases in temporary and part-time work
arrangements.

One particular finding of the earlier study by O'Brien
and Dillon is noteworthy. For the most part, it was the economically disadvantaged groups who secured the inferior
accommodation (where problems of overcrowding, sharing
and lack of facilities are most acute), paid the highest proportions of their incomes on rent and experienced the most
fears of eviction (p. 61). Of course, people on the margins

of the rental system in this manner are also most vulnerable to homelessness, and the survey confirmed that those in vulnerable situations of this kind (especially on low incomes and out of work) were heavily represented among the homeless population. The authors also pinpointed the poor standards of accommodation and the inadequate control over such standards. "The end result is that, with the exception of a small minority of new blocks of flats or new houses, there appears to be minimum control over standards of property coming onto the market for private rental accommodation" (O'Brien and Dillon, p. 20).

Despite an increase in the provision of private-rented accommodation in recent years (much of it influenced by the availability of tax incentives since the early 1980s which we examine below), significant difficulties remain, especially for private tenants. This has engendered many problems for tenants and is partly responsible for a generally negative perception of the rental option. In effect, the vulnerability, variable quality, and poor value for money associated with rental has meant that individuals and households regard it as a "tenure of last resort" (McCashin, 2000) and are encouraged to get out of this sector and into home ownership if at all possible.

The Housing (Miscellaneous Provisions) Act 1992 provided that a minimum period of written notice (28 days) to quit must be provided to a tenant, and this applied to all residential tenancies. The Act also provided for the making of regulations regarding standards of accommodation, the provision of rent books and registration by landlords. The regulations regarding standards and rent books were introduced in 1993 and those relating to registration in 1996. Landlords were obliged to ensure that rented houses or apartments complied with minimum standards relating to structural repair, sanitary facilities, heating, ventilation, cooking equipment, storage of food, electrical and gas fittings and equipment. The standards put considerable emphasis on health and safety considerations. The local authorities were given responsibility for ensuring that landlords complied with these standards, in practice through a system of inspections.

What have been the effects of this legislation and the introduction of regulations? It seems likely that houses or apartments built during the last decade (about 60,000 units) would indeed conform to the health and safety standards, although as we see later, there are serious concerns regarding the general quality of recently constructed units. The record in relation to standards in the other 80,000 units is much less satisfactory. In 1997, four years after the enactment of legislation on standards, 5,501 units were inspected, and 1,902 units (35 per cent) did not comply with minimum standards. In 1998, the findings were even worse – 2,710 units, or 53 per cent of those inspected, did not meet minimum standards. In 1998, a Threshold survey of 333 tenants established that between 65 and 80 per cent of requests to landlords regarding necessary repairs and maintenance had been ignored (Downey, 1998). A further study of rent supplement tenants by the Combat Poverty Agency in 1999 again found considerable evidence of unfit accommodation and disputes about necessary repairs (Guerin, 1999, p. 72). The most recent available data for 2004 showed that 2,106 units (29 per cent of those inspected) were in breach of regulations (Department of Environment, Heritage and Local Government, 2005). If this sample is representative, it would imply that (assuming the 60,000 units built since 1991 are in compliance) over 23,000 units in the private rental system do not meet the minimum standards. Such a possibility is surely an alarming state of affairs.

Apart from safety considerations, much of the private rental accommodation – even the new units – can be regarded as unsatisfactory in terms of size, overall quality and suitability for families and children. A study of residents in new housing in Dublin's inner city carried out by

MacLaran et al. (1995) showed that a sizable proportion of respondents were critical of the inadequate storage space inside and outside the dwelling, as well as the small size and poor ventilation of kitchens. Garden space was generally considered to be quite inadequate and the vast majority of respondents (70%) felt that the garden space was unsuitable for children. A government commissioned report by KPMG (1996) also established that a large proportion of residential units, including those in the rental sector, were small, consisting almost exclusively of either one or two bed apartments. Bathrooms and kitchens were likewise undersized, many with little natural light or ventilation. There was a lack of semi-public or private space external to the buildings and very few play areas for children. The KPMG report also expressed serious reservations regarding the lack of adequate storage space, the size of individual rooms and the absence of residential amenities. As well as the poor environmental conditions, KPMG argued that the existing guidelines regarding the size of units issued by the Department of the Environment in 1995 were unhelpful in allowing a large proportion of small residential units, in comparison with comparable guidelines in other European countries.

Despite these reservations, developers have persisted in constructing a large proportion of one and two bedroom apartments in Dublin's 'inner city', facilitated by both Dublin City Council and Dublin Docklands Development Authority on the grounds that there is a 'market' for such apartments, especially for investors. Kelly and MacLaran show that one-bed apartments built or with live planning permission in 2003 accounted for 37 per cent of all residential developments since 1996, while two-bedroom units accounted for a further 54 per cent (Kelly and MacLaran, 2004). In Dublin Docklands it could be argued that this trend is in direct conflict with the stated aim in the Docklands *Master Plan* to build a range of house types, including family units (Dublin Docklands Development Authority, 1997).

The requirement in the 1992 Act to provide tenants with rent books has apparently met with a high level of compliance. However, the regulations requiring registration by landlords was vigorously opposed for many years, and only 19 per cent of landlords had registered their rented units by March 2000 (Commission on the Private Rented Residential Sector, 2000). This situation persisted until recently when the new Private Residential Tenancies Board began to tackle the problem more proactively in 2005.

In short, the history of the private rental sector suggests that there has been a high level of non-compliance with regulations on standards and registration and, even worse, very low levels of enforcement by local authorities. Out of 1,902 units which did not meet minimum standards in 1997, only 8 legal cases were instigated. In 1998, no case was taken although 2,710 units were in breach of regulations. Even by the end of 2004 when 2,106 units were in breach of minimum standards, only 4 cases of enforcement were initiated. Apparently, the Department of the Environment has been repeatedly calling for tougher action by the local authorities to enforce regulations. It seems that these calls have largely fallen on deaf ears and a low priority has been given to this issue (op.cit., 2000, pp. 95-96).

TAX INCENTIVES IN THE PRIVATE RENTED SECTOR

As noted above, legislation enacted regarding rent books, registration of tenancies and standards of accommodation has met with mixed results. However, one initiative that has had a significant effect was the introduction of generous tax incentives by the government in "designated areas" of inner cities, seaside resorts and in many towns and villages throughout the country since 1981. These measures included a scheme to encourage the construction of rental accommodation for the general public and for students, another scheme designed to improve facilities in seaside resorts and a scheme to encourage residential development in the North West of the country – the Shannon corridor scheme. One of the best known and widely publicised schemes was called Section 23 after the relevant section of the Finance Act of 1981 which first introduced the tax incentive. The scheme was designed to encourage developers and builders to build houses and apartments for sale or for letting as by the early 1980s the number of units for letting had been declining for many years and there was a considerable need for such flexible, often short-term, accommodation. The scheme gave landlords or owner occupiers generous tax allowances (equivalent to the cost of the property minus the site value) over a period of ten years. Landlords could offset the cost of the property as a tax allowance against rents received from such properties as well as rent from any other rental properties they owned. By any measure, the tax incentive was very generous. As a result, a range of residential accommodation was built in areas which had previously been neglected or avoided altogether by the building industry and by the business community in general. It should be acknowledged, moreover, that the scheme had a positive physical effect in many areas. However, while designed as a short-term measure, mainly to encourage an increase in rented residential accommodation, the scheme was subsequently retained with minor amendment in Section 27 of the Finance Act of 1988. Since then, its abolition was proposed on numerous occasions, but it has been retained ever since on an ad hoc basis by successive Ministers for Finance. In the December 2004 Budget, the current Minister for Finance, Mr. Brian Cowen, proposed an evaluation of this and other schemes to assess their impact and the possible negative effects if they were to be abolished.

The Pilot Tax Relief Scheme for the Renewal and Improvement of Certain Resort Areas (commonly known as the Seaside Resort Scheme) was introduced in July 1995 for three years on a pilot basis. The qualifying period was extended in the Finance Act of 1998 for a further year. Over 5,000 houses were built over a three-year period in 15 major seaside resorts throughout the country, including Courtown, Tramore, Youghal, Clonakilty, Ballybunion, Lahinch and Galway. Designed to improve accommodation in seaside resorts and to attract more visitors, the scheme again offered significant tax allowances to investors, whereby expenditure could be offset against all other income. While investors were, under the regulations, required to let the properties for up to ten years, it transpired that many properties were not in fact rented in the normal way and simply reverted to "holiday homes", vacant for most of the year.

Such schemes have a number of serious flaws. First, they increase the demand for qualifying housing or apartments, as well as land, especially among potential landlords, investors and speculators who plan to let the properties even on short-term basis before selling on in order to realise a capital gain. Consequently, these groups are therefore in competition for housing with first time buyers or others who wish to set up a home. Landlords and investors are invariably willing and able to pay higher prices, particularly if they envisage further price increases. In any case, the availability of the tax incentives gives an unfair advantage to this group over the aspiring buyer who wishes to establish a home. Furthermore, as shown in Chapter 3, many of these properties now lie vacant in towns and villages around the country and are not fulfilling the intention of the original legislation. Despite this, their owners can claim tax relief on rental income received from other investment properties, while contemplating a significant capital gain on the vacant houses which will attract the current low capital gains tax.

The tax incentive schemes are also inherently regressive since they can only benefit those with sufficient incomes to incur tax liability. Those who have low incomes are disqualified from availing of such tax avoidance schemes since they do not have the necessary capital to become investors in property development in the designated areas or to become owner occupiers once the schemes are completed. This problem has generated conflict in recent years both in the inner city areas and in seaside towns, where the local populations find themselves excluded from the benefits and even 'displaced' as the escalating land and house prices make it impossible for their children to purchase a home in the local area.

A further problem with such schemes is that they are very costly indeed in terms of tax foregone. The Tax Strategy Group in the Department of Finance has done some estimates of this tax forgone on a range of incentives, although a lack of data has made it impossible at this point to isolate the precise cost of Section 23/27. However, the total tax forgone on capital allowances, including business allowances and those associated with urban and rural tax schemes (where Section 23/27 are important elements) amounted to €1.9 billion in 2001 alone (Tax Strategy Group, Department of Finance, 2004). The Seaside Resort Scheme alone cost an estimated €319 million over a four-year period (see Table 4.6).

While there may have been reasonable arguments for the introduction of such tax schemes in the 1980s when economic activity was very sluggish, it is now clear that they are inequitable and furthermore contribute in a most undesirable manner to house price inflation. As such, it would be very difficult to justify the continuance of such schemes. In contrast, the tax relief afforded to private tenants continues to be very modest in comparison with the groups mentioned above. Indeed, tenants have been largely neglected, in stark contrast to the situation in a range of European countries.

Table 4.6 Estimated Tax Cost of Seaside Resort Scheme, 1995-99

Resort	€ million
Achill	16.5
Arklow	7.6
Ballybunion	6.4
Bundoran	38.4
Clogherhead	2.5
Clonakilty	10.0
Courtown	52.0
Enniscrone	23.0
Kilkee	25.0
Lahinch	13.0
Laytown/ Bettystown/ Mosney	8.9
Salthill, Galway	24.0
Tramore	22.0
Westport	24.0
Youghal	46.0
TOTAL	319.3

Source: Reply by Minister for Finance to Dail Question, 6 October 2005, Ref. 27296/05

RECENT PROPOSED REFORM: THE COMMISSION REPORT AND NEW LEGISLATION

In view of widespread concern over many years regarding the difficulties in the private rented sector the government agreed in June 1999 to establish a Commission on the Private Rented Residential Sector with a view to :

(a) improving the security of tenure of tenants,
(b) maintaining a fair and reasonable balance between the respective rights and obligations of landlords and tenants, and

(c) increasing investment in, and supply of, residential accommodation for renting, including the removal of any identified constraints to the development of the sector.

The Commission had strong representation from government departments, from auctioneering and other property interests, as well as experts on investments and legal matters. Threshold and the St Vincent de Paul Society were the main representatives of tenant interests. In his introduction to the Report, the Chairman of the Commission (2000) signalled the difficulties of reaching consensus:

> Inevitably there was conflict during the work of the Commission and, also inevitably, solutions recommended will not fully meet all the requirements of the interests involved. Nor will they fully meet the heartfelt demands of those who have different views about the way society should order the relationship between residential landlords and tenants. In some cases, this is impossible, because these demands are born of differing philosophical and political views about the relative rights and responsibilities of those who provide accommodation to the sector and those who rent it. (p. i).
>
> The core issue of giving a right to tenants to continue in occupation, with a degree of certainty about rent levels, for an extended period proved the most difficult for the Commission. On this issue proposals were adopted by majority vote and some members opposed the particular solution recommended …Clearly it is regrettable that a consensus was not reached (p. ii).

Therefore, the report of the Commission was, as the Chairman put it, "the result of much compromise between the various interests" (p. ii).

Allowing for this challenging process of negotiation (itself a fascinating manifestation of the different philosophies of housing set out in Chapter 2), what were the conclusions of the Commission in relation to the "core issues" of security of tenure and rent certainty? One majority recommendation was to implement a limited form of security of tenure. It proposed that where a tenancy lasted for a minimum continuous period of six months, the tenant would then be entitled to continue in occupation for another three and a half years. The tenancy could, with 28 days notice, be terminated without reason by the landlord during the first six months. The landlord could also gain re-possession during the protected period for a range of stated reasons. In relation to rent, the Commission recommended an "open market rent" and that rent should not be subject to review more frequently than once per annum, unless there was substantial change in the nature of the accommodation.

Three organisations represented on the Commission disagreed with the above majority view: Threshold, St. Vincent de Paul and the Union of Students in Ireland. Threshold put it as follows:

> Threshold is of the view that the range of recommendations proposed by the Commission in relation to security of tenure, rent regulation and affordability will not result in a fundamental and necessary reform of the private rented sector and will not result in a substantial immediate benefit to tenants
>
> The absence of any proposals for rent regulation is an inadequate response to the situation where significant numbers of tenants face substantial annual rent increases (pp 169-170).

As outlined in this report, the Irish Property Owners' Association (IPOA) opposed even the limited right to occupation by a tenant for up to four years:

> Investors will recognize this automatic right to occupy as

> an encumbrance on the property rights of the
> provider...this new property right will be open to abuse by
> unscrupulous tenants. (p. 166)

The majority of the Commission recommended the establishment of a Private Residential Tenancies Board to deal
with a range of disputes, to provide information to landlords and tenants, to register landlords and to encourage
good practice. The Irish Property Owners Association
strongly opposed the range of powers proposed for the
Board:

> The IPOA believes that the Residential Tenancies Board
> should deal solely with dispute resolution. In reality this is
> the creation of a statutory agency to oversee the entire
> rental accommodation sector. (p. 166)

The IPOA also opposed the proposal that landlords should
have to register all tenancies on the grounds that it constituted "an unreasonable burden on landlords" (p. 166).

The Residential Tenancies Act 2004 largely reflected the
majority view of the Commission. The Act specifies that a
landlord can terminate a tenancy without giving a reason,
during the first six months. A tenancy will hereafter normally hold for a further three and a half years. However, a
landlord can terminate a tenancy during this latter period
for a range of specified grounds such as failure by the tenant to comply with his/her obligations under the tenancy,
proposed sale of the dwelling, occupation by the landlord
or a member of his/her family or substantial refurbishment. While an improvement on the existing situation,
these loopholes would seem to provide relatively easy
routings to secure an eviction if a landlord so wishes, such
that the security of tenure afforded some tenants may still
be notional. Moreover, at the end of each tenancy the
occupant is once again subject to a six month probationary

period and therefore may be evicted relatively easily.

The 2004 Act, as expected, specifies that the rent payable by a tenant shall not be greater than the "market rent" and rent shall be reviewed no more than once per annum, unless a substantial refurbishment has occurred (Sections 19-20). The "market rent" is defined as "the rent which a willing tenant not already in occupation would give and a willing landlord would take for the dwelling, in each case on the basis of vacant possession and having regard to the letting values of dwellings of a similar size, type and character to the dwelling and situated in a comparable area" (Section 24). While this is, in effect, a form of "second generation" rent regulation, the rent proposed is not really a "market rent" since it does not reflect the interaction of demand and supply between many tenants and landlords to determine that rent. Rather, rent would apparently be agreed between landlord and tenant without any competition and the landlord would obviously be in the strongest negotiating position. Secondly, there is no formal provision for regulating the extent of rent increases which is a central element of second generation rent regulation, as discussed earlier. Most EU countries have moved towards a system that allows some type of rent indexation to consumer price inflation. Thus, the typical rental contract in the EU includes an indexation clause that refers to the consumer price index. In Denmark, Sweden and France, indexation is linked to housing costs. Germany has an adjustment mechanism that allows increases in rents of sitting tenants up to a maximum of 20 per cent over three years (European Central Bank, 2003).

If rents were set at levels which did not allow a reasonable profit on investment (as happened in the past in Dublin when rents were controlled at unreasonably low levels), landlords would inevitably allow properties to deteriorate or dispose of them, hence reducing supply. If, however, rents were indexed to allow "normal" profits to be made, landlords would be unlikely to transfer to other enterprises. The best known example of similar regulation was the price control of alcohol some years ago. While owners of licensed premises were unhappy with such control, none appeared to go out of business and the measure certainly did not reduce the supply of alcohol. It is absurd to suggest that a "fair rent" (which provides for a "normal" profit) could militate unreasonably against landlords and hence reduce the supply of rental accommodation further. Rather, fair rents, allied to greater certainty regarding the size of rental payments, are in the interests of both landlords and tenants. In an Irish context, it is significant that the principle and legitimacy of rent regulation was in fact acknowledged by the Commission:

> ...the Commission is of the view that there is no existing constitutional or legal impediment to recommending the introduction of a system of rent control, provided that such a system was framed within the context of the common good and was fair and not oppressive, paying due regard to the rights and interests of both parties (pp. 110-111)

One of the most important initiatives in the 2004 Act was the establishment of the Private Rental Tenancies Board recommended by the Commission. Although the Board has only commenced its work in 2005, its potential is enormous in relation to resolving disputes regarding the so-called "market rents", standards of accommodation, security of tenure and return of deposits. Whether the Board has the resources and determination to deal with the undoubted challenges in the private rented sector remains to be seen.

PRIVATE RENTAL AS PUBLIC HOUSING PROVIDER?

As a partial consequence of tenure restructuring in the 1990s, particularly the under-development of social housing relative to needs, the private rental sector has increasingly been turned to as an alternative source of social housing (see also Punch, 2005). This development has been facilitated under the Supplementary Welfare Allowance (SWA) scheme, which is now an important policy approach to low-income housing provision. The SWA, which came into operation on 1 July 1977 to replace the home assistance service, was designed to provide income support to households whose means were insufficient to meet their needs. The rent supplement component of SWA, which also provides basic income maintenance, mortgage supplements, heating and diet supplements, exceptional needs and urgent needs payments and the back to school clothing and footwear scheme, was originally intended as a source of short-term assistance (e.g. while seeking employment) to help people meet the cost of renting. However, this model has taken on, in ad-hoc fashion, a broader more deeply embedded social role in the housing system: "Originally, SWA rent supplement was designed as a residual means of income support to provide immediate and short-term assistance with unmet needs. Nonetheless it has become, almost by default, a mainstream housing income support" (Guerin, 1999, p. 83).

This is borne out by the striking escalation in expenditure on the scheme, as well as the fact that a majority of households receiving rent supplements have been on the scheme for more than 12 months. In a study of SWA recipients, over 12 per cent of respondents had been receiving rent supplements at their present accommodation for over four years (Guerin, 1999). Moreover, it is estimated that one-third of all private rented households are receiving rent supplement (Fahey and Watson, 1995; Guerin, 1999).

Although it has clearly become a mainstream social housing model, the SWA is weakly situated within the rubric of housing policy, being funded by the Department of Social and Family Affairs but administered by the Health Boards through their community welfare service. Furthermore, its intended role has not been clearly articulated, and it represents in some senses a disjointed response to low-income housing needs, particularly since many of those dependent on it do not feature in the assessments of housing needs (Fahey and Watson, 1995; Guerin, 1999).

Nevertheless, positive as well as negative features of this approach have been identified. Most importantly it offers a relatively rapid response to housing needs once it is established, at least in comparison to the lengthy waits increasingly typical of local authority housing. Furthermore, it is the *only* housing option open to many marginalised people[2], such as single-person households, who often have difficulty accessing public waiting lists, despite being on a low income and in real need. A further positive is that accommodation available is often in relatively accessible locations in urban areas (e.g. inner city, inner suburbs).

A number of problems are immediately apparent, however. The quality of accommodation has tended to be modest in general and quite poor in some instances, although this will vary from area to area depending on the practices of the relevant community welfare officer (many aspects of the SWA scheme are applied on a discretionary basis). Despite this, the cost of accommodation being subsidised under the scheme has also increased considerably over the years from €7.8 million in 1989 to €354 million in 2004 (Department of Social and Family Affairs, 2005). Prospective recipients of this income support must first establish a tenancy, and they may experience considerable difficulty in doing so. This also leaves people open to the possibility of discrimination. Although this housing option is often seen as affording greater choice (at least in comparison to the residualised social rental system), in reality, disadvantaged households may struggle to access suitable accommodation, particularly during times of scarcity. Guerin's (1999) study, for instance, shows that choice in accommodation was limited, 42 per cent of respondents describing their dwelling as "all that was available", while for 17 per cent it was simply the "cheapest available". Also of relevance here is the finding that 66 per cent experienced some difficulty in finding a landlord who would accept SWA (including 52 per cent who had a high level of difficulty). A recent survey of rent supplement tenants in Cork confirmed the continuation of these various difficulties (Threshold, 2005). Further difficulties emerged from a decision at the end of 2002 to increase tenant contributions to the rent (i.e. from their social welfare payment) from €6 to €12 per week and to limit the maximum rent allowable in different geographic areas (e.g. a limit of €107 per week was set for single people in Dublin). A policy change was made in 2004 which disqualified households from SWA unless they had a tenancy for at least six months. However, this was later seen to create hardship for many households and an appropriate amendment was made.

CONCLUSION

Reform in the privately rented housing sector is long overdue in the interests of both landlords and tenants. The impact of the new Private Residential Tenancies Act 2004 and the new Residential Tenancies Board remains to be seen. In any case, it seems clear that a privately rented sector which offers "fair rents" (indexed for inflation and relevant improvements), good quality and reasonable security of tenure (as is the case in many other countries) could play a useful role in the housing system, to meet a range of needs. However, regular inspections of rental accommodation and resolute action to ensure quality control and adherence to agreements should be the norm. This would be in the interests of both landlords and tenants and would encourage the provision of a wider range of rental accommodation in the long term. The use of the private rented sector as a "public housing provider" raises fundamental questions as to whether this is good value for money and whether the significant sums expended would be better spent on the provision of public housing, a major problem which we turn to in Chapter 5.

Notes

1   One in five in the private rental sector exceeded the "affordability" threshold in 1999-2000. See Fahey, Nolan and Maitre, 2004.
2. The term marginalised is used here because the scheme excludes those in full time but low-wage employment (the working poor) as well as those in full-time education

Chapter 5

Public Housing:
The Poor Relation?

In view of the difficulties outlined in the previous chapters in purchasing a home or renting one in the private rented sector, it is inevitable that many people turn to the Local Authorities or other not-for-profit organisations in the hope of securing an affordable home. It seems clear that many individuals or couples who might originally aspire to purchase or rent on the market are now simply unable to do so. They lack the "ability to pay", which is of course the critical prerequisite for participation in the market. This affordability problem across the market sector has broader implications, including increasing need for public provision. Worst of all is the plight of the most marginalised households who find it increasingly difficult to get into the private rental sector, even at the bottom end, due to increasing demand and escalating rents further up the ladder from higher-income groups who have postponed or given up altogether on the attempt to purchase a home. This "crowding out" effect noted earlier has the immediate consequence of a higher level of unmet housing need and greater vulnerability to homelessness.

THE EXTENT OF HOUSING NEED

Under Section 9 of the Housing Act, 1988 each Local Authority is required to carry out a periodic assessment of need. Housing need is defined as the number requiring housing due to a range of "personal' factors e.g. unable to afford, existing accommodation over-crowded or unfit, currently homeless, elderly. Using this definition, the trend in housing need is set out in Table 5.1.

Table 5.1 Number of Households in Housing Need, 1993-2002

Category of need	1993	1996	1999	2002
Unable to afford	6,432	7,659	13,328	21,452
Unfit accommodation	5,122	4,799	4,796	4,065
Overcrowded	7,075	5,912	8,328	8,513
Involuntary sharing	3,345	3,120	4,086	4,421
Leaving institutional care	68	66	67	82
Medical	1,861	1,762	2,347	3,400
Elderly	2,191	2,140	2,363	2,006
Disability	194	241	236	423
Homeless	1,452	979	2,219	2,468
Travellers	884	749	1,406	1,583
TOTAL	28,624	27,427	39,176	48,413

Source: *Housing Statistics Bulletin,* 1993–2002

This Table shows that the number of households in need dropped from 28,624 households in 1993 to 27,427 in 1996 with almost all categories registering decline. However, as was illustrated earlier, house prices began to escalate from the mid 1990s and private rents followed the same pattern. Not surprisingly, the numbers who were unable to procure affordable and appropriate accommodation increased significantly over a few years. Between 1996 and 1999 the number of households defined as being in need increased by 12,000 and by a further 9,200 by 2002. This represented about 140,000 people for whom the Celtic Tiger economic boom had done little. Table 5.2 shows that over the ten year period significant increases took place in Dublin (6,807 households) and Cork (1,066 households) although Galway registered the greatest proportionate change (178 per cent increase). The County Councils and Borough/Urban District Councils each recorded increases in housing need by over 5,000 households. We should note, however, that there has been considerable debate concerning the extent of housing need. Some argue that the 48,400 households in Table 5.2 is an over-estimate; others suggest that the real figure could be much higher (see O'Sullivan, 2004, for a useful discussion).

Table 5.2 Main Areas of Housing Need,
1993 and 2002

Cities	1993	2002	Change	% Change
Cork	1,216	2,282	+1,066	87.7
Dublin	7,890	14,897	+6,807	86.3
Galway	475	1,320	+845	177.9
Limerick	568	581	+13	2.3
Waterford	683	1,034	+351	51.4
Total	10,832	19,914	+9,082	83.8
Co. Councils	11,700	16,978	+5,278	45.1
Boroughs and urban districts	6,092	11,521	+5,429	89.1
Total	28,624	48,413	+19,789	69.1

Source: *Housing Statistics Bulletin*, 1993-2002

We believe, however, that the total extent of housing need is likely to be much higher than the official estimate for a number of reasons. Consider, first, the high proportions of people for whom homes are officially regarded as unaffordable (i.e. more than 35 per cent of net income would have to be spent on mortgage payments), as discussed in Chapter 3. For example, the proportion of such households was estimated to be as high as 50 per cent in parts of Dublin, with the national figure at 33 per cent. By definition, this group should enter the category of housing need. Taking the national figure, this group comprises about 14,000 households (about 41,000 persons) per annum over the period up to 2006. Consider then, as pointed out in Chapter 4, the large number of low-income households receiving rent supplement in the private rented sector – estimated to be between 50,000 and 60,000 at any one time. In 2004, about 58,000 were receiving rent supplement, of which 14,500 were on Local Authority waiting lists and thereby already included in the first official category above. The remaining 43,500 households, however, can arguably be classified as being in housing need since rent supplement cannot realistically represent a long-term housing solution for them. Indeed, the proposal by government in July 2004 to establish by 2007 a Rental Accommodation Scheme (RAS), with an emphasis on providing long-term accommodation to replace rent supplement, is an official, if belated, recognition that rent supplement is an unsatisfactory approach.

We argue that a more realistic picture of housing need is arrived at by adding these two latter estimates to the official estimate of housing need of 48,400. (See Table 5.3) Our estimate comes to a total of 106,000 households (many of them single persons on rent supplement) or some 250,000 people who are likely to be currently in housing need. This calculation does not, of course, take into account all elements of categories such as homeless persons, refugees, or those with disabilities who may be inappropriately housed or have no home at all, but are not yet officially counted. Nor does it take account of the significant increase in population and extra household formation likely to take place into the future. Whether we take the official estimate of housing need or our own estimate from Table 5.3, we would argue that the current public provision is inadequate to meet either current or future requirements.

Table 5.3. New Estimate of Housing Need, 2005

	Households	Persons
1. Official Assessment 2002	48,400	140,000*
2. Housing Strategies Estimate 2001-2002	14,000	41,000**
3. Rent Supplement Tenants 2004	43,500	69,000***
Total	105,900	250,000

Notes:
* Assuming average household size
** The estimate for one year only. Therefore likely under-estimate since 2001.
*** We are assuming 18,000 single-person households. Other households consist of two or more people. We have assumed only two persons per household, so that the above is an under-estimate of the real total.

PUBLIC HOUSING PROVISION AND SALES

The most obvious way to tackle housing need is to construct housing via the Local Authorities, Housing Associations or other not-for-profit organisations. The record of Local Authority provision over the eleven years is given in Table 5.4. Provision is made up of newly-built houses and those acquired by the Local Authority at market prices. The gross gain in the stock over the period in question was 43,253 homes or an average of 3,932 per annum. However, this gain was counteracted by the sales of Local

Authority houses to sitting tenants at a significant discount. Sales amounted to 17,809 over the period or 1,619 per annum. The net gain was thus only 25,444 homes or an average of only 2,313 per annum since 1994. It should be noted that an average of about 3,700 local authority houses become vacant each year. While these are obviously helpful in accommodating new or transfer tenants, they are not a net addition to the housing stock.[1]

Table 5.4 Local Authority Housing Provision and Sales, 1994-2004

	Constructed	Acquired	Total Gain	Sales	Net Gain
1994	2,374	467	2,841	505	2,336
1995	2,960	882	3,842	950	2,892
1996	2,676	897	3,573	2,284	1,289
1997	2,632	585	3,217	2,139	1,078
1998	2,771	511	3,282	2,006	1,276
1999	2,909	804	3,713	2,256	1,457
2000	2,204	1,003	3,207	1,844	1,363
2001	3,622	1,400	5,022	1,411	3,611
2002	4,403	671	5,074	1,195	3,879
2003	4,516	456	4,972	1,567	3,405
2004	3,539	971	4,510	1,652	2,858
Total 1994 -2004	34,606	8,647	43,253	17,809	25,444

Source: *Housing Statistics Bulletins,* various years

In the light of the significant housing need outlined earlier, it would be difficult to justify a continuation of the sales of local authority housing. It would be most unwise to continue selling at significant discounts while at the same time purchasing at market prices, especially since tenants who wish to own homes can do so via several more appropriate routes e.g. affordable housing and shared ownership schemes. Such sales have resulted over the years in a sharp reduction in the local authority housing stock. A continuation of the sales scheme will result in the further residualisation of public housing whereby only the very low income or unemployed households will be in public rental. Furthermore, the loss of rental income means that a "maturation effect" which contributes to long-term viability will be lost.

In addition to Local Authority provision, a range of philanthropic bodies and Housing Associations, acting in co-operation with the Local Authorities, have been active for some years in building houses for rent. One early example of a philanthropic organisation was the Iveagh Trust established in 1890 by Sir Edward Cecil Guinness, First Earl of Iveagh (Aalen, 1990). The Trust is now recognised as a Housing Association and is active in hostel provision as well as building and refurbishing homes for the elderly and others in need. Housing Association accommodation is built with assistance of two important schemes – the Capital Assistance Scheme and the Capital Loan and Subsidy Scheme – both administered by the Department of the Environment and Local Government. The Associations usually focus on small local communities and cater for a proportion of low-income tenants who cannot get onto Local Authority lists. However, those on the waiting lists receive priority for most of the houses. The provision by Housing Associations over the past ten years is given in Table 5.5. For most of the period they provided less than 1,000 homes per annum (largely due to difficulties of funding as well as land acquisition and land prices), but with increased support from government their output has increased significantly in recent years and rose to 1,600 homes during both 2003 and 2004. Apart from performing a most useful role in housing provision, some Housing Associations have given attention to broader community facilities and have been successful in relation to housing management in association with their tenants. It may be noted, however, that Associations under current legislation cannot become involved in tenant purchase schemes on the grounds that this would reduce further the stock of badly-needed homes.

Table 5.5 Voluntary and Co-operative Housing Provision, 1994-2004

Year	Capital Assistance Scheme	Capital Loan and Subsidy Scheme	Total
1994	607	294	901
1995	613	398	1,011
1996	501	416	917
1997	345	411	756
1998	283	202	485
1999	314	265	579
2000	484	467	951
2001	554	699	1,253
2002	699	661	1,360
2003	1,018	599	1,617
2004	981	626	1,607
Total 1994-2004	6,399	5,038	11,437

Source: *Housing Statistics Bulletin*, various years

There are some concerns as to whether or not this sector can achieve the capacity hoped for by government. Official policy has envisaged a much greater role for voluntary associations in public housing provision since *A Plan for Social Housing* (Government of Ireland, 1991). This aspiration was reinforced in a practical way in the *National Development Plan*, which set a target for voluntary housing output of 4,000 dwellings per annum. While there has been some improvement since the NDP, the current output of 1,600 per annum is clearly a long way short of this target. There is also a continuing concern about how the sector should best be regulated, an increasingly important issue as it expands given the increased levels of public funding involved and the growing numbers of tenants affected (Brooke, 2001; Mullins et al., 2003).

We see from Tables 5.4 and 5.5 that Local Authorities and Housing Associations between them have provided an average net increase of 3,300 homes per annum over the last decade. Although this had increased to over 5,000 during 2002 and 2003, it fell to 4,400 in 2004 and this is still a modest performance in view of the large housing need illustrated earlier (see Hayden, 2004). The reasons for the poor record in the provision of public housing are complex, but they include the low priority given for many years to non-market provision in overall economic and social policy where some Local Authorities saw themselves as "enablers" or "facilitators" rather than direct providers. The problem was compounded in the past by the inadequate funding available from central government to Local Authorities and to other proven providers such as housing associations and co-operatives and the difficulties in acquiring land at a reasonable price. The Minister for the Environment has also argued that some local authorities have failed to utilise the funds allocated to them for housing provision (Roche, 2005).

Government Expenditure and Revenue: A Note

In view of the importance of housing it is useful to review briefly government expenditure and income. We draw here on calculations done for the NESC Report on housing in 2004 (NESC, 2004). Capital expenditure in 2003 amounted to €1,685 million. This included €858 million on new local authority housing as well as on improvements to existing homes, €210 million on the Capital Loan and Subsidy

Scheme and on the Capital Assistance Scheme, and smaller sums on new housing grants, affordable housing and other schemes. Current expenditure in 2003 on housing amounted to €428 million. Total expenditure was thus €2.1 billion. On the other hand, revenue related to housing was significant, including €1 billion from stamp duty, €1.8 billion from VAT on housing and €450 million in Part V contributions. Additional significant revenue accrues annually from capital gains tax, corporation tax on developers' profits, development contributions, income tax and local authority and affordable housing sales. In short, the government makes a significant net gain from housing.

THE HOMELESS

The most obvious housing problem in Ireland is exclusion from housing altogether – a problem faced by homeless people, for whom finding a place to stay with some measure of security or certainty is a very real and continuing crisis of everyday life. Homelessness is a complex issue, arising from a range of problems with which people may be faced at some time in their lives, including economic hardship, de-institutionalisation, personal crises, family breakdown, psychiatric illnesses, intellectual disability, and drug or alcohol abuse. The experience of homelessness leaves people vulnerable to ill health, while making it almost impossible to secure employment. In all kinds of ways, therefore, to be homeless is to be marginalised, to exist on the very edge of society.

The Extent of the Problem

The Housing Act (1988) set out a definition of homelessness and required local authorities to assess the number of homeless in their area. It also allowed local authorities to offer accommodation to homeless people and to set aside a particular number or proportion of dwellings for such purposes. Since the Act was enacted, five assessments of homelessness have been carried out (and a sixth is underway at the time of writing). The most recent available assessment provided an estimate of 5,581 persons (4,176 adults and 1,405 children). As shown in Table 5.6, the official homeless estimate has more than doubled since 1993, the major growth ironically taking place in the "boom" years from 1996 to 1999. On the basis of these figures, the main problem occurs in the cities, particularly in the Dublin area, where the number of homeless increased by 146 per cent since 1993 and where in 2002 some 73 per cent of the national homeless population lived. While some questions can be raised concerning the accuracy of the data in earlier years (see, for example, O'Sullivan, 2004), it seems likely that the 2002 figure of 5,581 is a conservative estimate. This is supported by recent research involving a survey of eight local authorities (covering most of the main urban areas), the majority of whom stated that the homeless counts under-reported the extent of the problem (Bergin et al., 2005).

Table 5.6 The Homeless in Ireland, 1993-2002

Area	1993	1996	1999	2002	Absolute change, 1993-2002	% Change, 1993-2002
County councils	385	260	439	415	30	7.8
City councils	2,120	1,994	4,589	4,860	2,740	129.2
Of which Dublin	*1,648*	*1,533*	*3,918*	*4,060*	*2,412*	*146.4*
Borough Councils	33	70	76	72	39	118.2
Town Councils	129	177	130	234	105	81.4
TOTAL	2,667	2,501	5,234	5,581	2,914	109.3

Source: *Housing Statistics Bulletin,* various editions

The accuracy of the official count is also called into question by some odd trends. Many county councils and town councils recorded no homeless persons at all in 2002 despite having significant numbers in previous years. As an example, the number of homeless in Longford in 1999 was 103 persons; there were none in 2002! Were they all accommodated by Longford County Council (in which case it should publish its strategy for housing the homeless as a model of best practice) or did they all migrate to other areas? Moreover, in some counties, the Homeless Action Plan suggests a much larger figure than that in the official count, while homeless service provision is on a scale well above the level required if we are to believe the official assessment. In Clare, for example, the official assessment in 2002 recorded only two homeless people, but the Homeless Strategy made provision for 130. We conclude, therefore, that the 2002 assessment most likely under-estimates the extent of homelessness.

Many homeless people face considerable difficulties in getting back into permanent accommodation. Recent evidence suggests that people are homeless for longer periods than at the commencement of the Government's *Homelessness: An Integrated Strategy* in 2000. Furthermore, the average time spent by the homeless in emergency accommodation has increased from an average of only 20 days in 1993 to an average of 18 months in 2003. Research has also shown that even where homeless people are able to get onto local authority housing waiting lists,[2] they tend to face longer waiting times to get housed than other households – some local authorities reported typical wait times of two to six years (Bergin et al., 2005). Whatever the scale of homelessness might be at any point in time, it is unacceptable and the policy target must be to eliminate it by ensuring access to stable, permanent housing for all.

What Does it Mean to be Homeless?

At first glance, the term "homelessness" may appear reasonably unproblematic. However, there are different views as to what constitutes "being homeless". Although the public in general holds fairly graphic images of what this state constitutes, where "homelessness" begins and ends is less easily agreed. In effect, this is a contested term, and the meaning and importance attached to it by people in different situations – social service providers, social activists, government officials, civil servants, academics, people living in shelters, people living beside existing or proposed shelters – vary significantly. This problem was also highlighted in the study by Bergin et al. (2005), which found evidence that there is no commonly agreed definition of what constitutes homelessness across local authorities, homeless persons units and voluntary organisations. This is a problem of language in part, but it is also politicised in that different definitions will, variously, understate or overstate the extent and urgency of the problem. The obvious practical problem lies in monitoring levels of homelessness without agreement as to what this "condition" denotes. Notoriously, for instance, some methodologies for counting rough sleepers require people to be literally asleep on the streets as opposed to sitting up against a wall wrapped in a blanket and having a chat which disqualifies one's claim to be a rough sleeper.

These problems of definition have been explored in detail by (among others) FEANTSA (the European Federation of National Organisations working with the homeless) in a number of studies (Edgar et al., 1999, 2000). To begin with, there are legal definitions, which tend to be very limiting, highlighting priority cases, but omitting many people who are without a place to call home. Not surprisingly, many social workers, health professionals, housing advocates and others working in the field do not readily accept such definitions.

Others take a relative view, emphasising people's access to minimal 'levels' of housing and security in their accommodation. Thus, homelessness is viewed across a continuum from sleeping rough through emergency accommodation (including hostels and B&Bs) or institutions to inadequate accommodation (overcrowded, involuntary sharing, sub-standard). Here the policy challenge acknowledges the need for more than "shelter" (a roof over one's head) – there is also a need to attend to people's diverse and complex social and health requirements and to seek to help people move from emergency to supported to independent and stable accommodation solutions.

There is also a debate about the individual versus the societal viewpoint. Some observers who emphasise individual culpability and responsibility, see homelessness as a marginal problem experienced by more or less deviant people or even as a "lifestyle choice". This viewpoint is underpinned by a philosophical perspective that emphasises individualism and the role of market systems, while downplaying the role of the state and the legitimacy of intervention. This is a view of society without solidarity or compassion, viewing both affluence and poverty as people's "just desserts" – a view taken to the extreme by Margaret Thatcher who infamously propounded that there is no society, only individuals. Indeed, authorities that adopt such a philosophy may well view homelessness as a criminal justice issue rather than as a matter for social policy. In short, people on the streets are essentially vagrants and need to be controlled or moved on, not least because the problem creates an image that is bad for business.

In contrast a more critical analytical approach would highlight the complex social relations that underpin and sustain homelessness. Among other concerns, this standpoint demands that we explore the structural disadvantage of households in vulnerable housing situations and the processes that tend to generate or perpetuate homelessness.

The problem in this view must be understood at least in part in terms of the effective marginalisation of individuals or social groups from full participation in society, including exclusion from adequate housing. Homelessness is thus a stark reflection of this deeper problem of social inequality and disempowerment; in a sense, it exists in the shadow of privilege and affluence. Resolving the problem would thus require more fundamental structural changes (e.g. changing the way housing is produced and allocated or addressing economic inequalities and social disadvantage) as well as short-term service supports or emergency responses.

The reality is that homelessness is, in some respects, a crisis of personal circumstances, requiring responses targeted at the individual level (and different individuals will require a diverse range of supports to progress), but it is also a crisis of social exclusion at the societal level, requiring fundamental structural interventions, including housing. Thus, emergency services and supports are necessary, but resolving the issue requires a broader approach, one that recognises the links between homelessness and the operation of the total housing system (as well as the interconnection between difficulties across all tenures) and commits to policy change to rectify the systemic failures.

The diversity of processes that produce and reproduce homelessness can be clarified by distinguishing the most frequent *causes* of homelessness in the first instance and the main reasons why people *remain* homeless once they are out of home. A recent study on *Drug Use Among the Homeless Population in Ireland* prepared by Merchants Quay Ireland for the National Advisory Committee on Drugs (Lawless and Corr, 2005) shows, for example, the relevance of both personal and structural factors. Importantly, the study clarifies that while many personal predicaments can lead to people ending up out of home (e.g. family conflict, drug and alcohol use), structural factors were in fact more important in understanding why people remain homeless

(Table 5.7). Put simply, the essential factors underlying the experience of homelessness relate primarily to barriers to procuring a home in Ireland. Similarly, a recent assessment of the impact of the Housing Act (1988) and *Homelessness: An Integrated Strategy* (2000) concluded that without dealing with the problem of access to long-term, stable housing, virtually no supportive intervention for homeless people works (Bergin et al., 2005). It should also be remembered that the situation regarding the relative importance of personal and structural factors is complicated when one considers that drug abuse, which can be a contributory factor to homelessness, is itself also in part a structural issue insofar as there is a well-known direct link between problem drug use and poverty (see for example Lawless and Cox, 2000; Ministerial Task Force, 1996, 1997).

Table 5.7 Main Reasons for Remaining Homeless

Reasons	Per Cent
Cannot access local authority housing	25
Cannot access private rental housing	11
Money problems	11
Continuing drug use	11
Continuing alcohol use	7
Family conflict	9
Personal choice	5
Other	21

Source: National Advisory Committee on Drugs, 2005

To a large extent, this line of analysis, emphasising the relative definition of homelessness and its structural as well as personal basis, is as a rule accepted (and acted on) by many working in the field. Voluntary organisations working with homeless people in Ireland generally tend towards a relative definition of homelessness, while also recognising the need for challenges to policy and structural disadvantage as well as service provision. Focus Ireland, for example, includes three categories in its definition of homeless (O'Sullivan, 1996):

- *Visible Homeless*: those sleeping rough and/or those accommodated in emergency shelters or Bed and Breakfasts
- *Hidden Homeless*: those families or individuals involuntarily sharing with family and friends, those in insecure accommodation or those living in housing that is woefully inadequate or sub-standard
- *At risk of Homelessness*: those who currently have housing but are likely to become homeless due to economic difficulties, too high a rent burden, insecure tenure or health difficulties.

Focus Ireland also reminds us of an important point about human dignity and the labels and prejudices sometimes attached to those marginalised by wider society:

People who are without a home find the label 'homeless' difficult to accept. They feel the stigma of homelessness very acutely and they feel that the word 'homeless' carries much of that stigma with it.

The word they use themselves to describe their period of homelessness is 'out': 'When I was out', 'We were out for nearly a year'. This expression is less offensive to the people undergoing the experience, and it suggests that the experience is not permanent, that they have a home somewhere that they eventually will be able to go back to, or that they have some chance of making a new home for themselves some day.

It is difficult to avoid the word 'homeless' altogether,

but in Focus Ireland we try to respect customers' feelings about this word and to use 'out-of-home' in preference to 'homeless' when we can (Focus Ireland, 2005)

Similarly, for the Simon Community, "homelessness is about more than just being without a roof or a house. It is about lack of shelter, lack of security, lack of belonging, and lack of safety". There is thus a need to adopt a relative concept of the problem (i.e. as a matter of degrees of vulnerability and exclusion from housing), something that is clarified when one considers where homeless people stay:

> "Sleeping rough" in doorways, in parks, on derelict sites, and in abandoned cars is the most extreme form of homelessness. But street homelessness is just the tip of iceberg. Many people who are homeless live in emergency accommodation: in shelters, hostels, or refuges. Others stay in B&Bs or "double-share" with friends and relatives. Sometimes, because of a lack of alternative options, people have to live long-term in such accommodation (Simon Communities of Ireland, 2005)

This understanding underlines the importance of entering into a broader social analysis of the problem – it is not sufficient to view it in terms of individual behaviour or deviancy (*ibid*):

> Homelessness is not something that happens in isolation. It is an extreme form of poverty and social exclusion. There are many factors that interact to cause or prolong homelessness. They include:
>
> - inadequate income
> - educational deprivation
> - involuntary emigration
> - low pay
> - unemployment

- family breakdown
- personal crisis such as an illness, a bereavement, or an addiction
- experience of institutional care
- lack of access to affordable housing

These are all urgent issues demanding serious concern and action given the implications:

> Long-term homelessness lowers the morale and self-esteem of people, often leading to depression. It has disastrous effects on their physical and mental health. Skin diseases, chronic bronchitis, alcoholism, emphysema, and TB are some of the severe medical problems suffered by a significant number of homeless people. Many homeless people do not live to see old age (*ibid*).

It is perhaps the loss of self-esteem and of dignity that is the most painful aspect of homelessness and marginalisation in general (something that again raises hard questions about the moral framework of our society and the market model on which there is so much emphasis). Indeed the readily apparent fact that access to housing is one of the most important social pre-conditions to ensure the realisation of people's dignity and potential underlines more forcefully the urgency of these issues. Drawing from his experience of working with marginalised and homeless youths for over 30 years in the north-east inner city of Dublin, Peter McVerry SJ makes this most important social and ethical dimension of the issue abundantly clear:

> I used to think that the hardest thing about being homeless was not having a bed to sleep in – having to find a doorway, or a derelict building, or the back of an abandoned car to lay your head. But I learnt from the young people that I am working with that that is not the hardest part of being homeless. So I thought it was the boredom, having nothing

to do, all day, every day; walking up and down trying the pass the time. But that is not the hardest part. Now I believe that the hardest part of being homeless is to live with the knowledge that if you disappeared off the face of the earth, no-one would even notice. That defines the value of your life. You are of no value to anyone, there is no-one to whom you are important, no-one who really cares. Your life is virtually meaningless. The message you receive from society, every minute of every day, is that you are not worth the trouble or effort or expense of providing you with even a small bedsit that you can call home (McVerry, 2003, p. 20).

Thus, the lack of accommodation is only the tip of the iceberg in understanding what homelessness means. To be homeless is to feel forgotten, ignored, uncared for, depersonalised, rootless, and without hope:

> To be homeless is to ask yourself *'why bother to keep going?'* *'What is the point of it all?'* You think that maybe you would be better off dead. Your life has no meaning, no value, no significance. If you were to die, no-one would even notice, you can't think of anyone who would miss you.
>
> To be homeless is to live your life *in the shadows*. In the shadows there is little light, little sun, little warmth. You look out at all those who are busy, rushing here and there, with things to do, people to meet, money to spend; they live in the brightness, where the sun shines and laughter can be heard. But between you and them there is a gulf which prevents you from getting from your side to theirs. And you ask *'Why?'* and no answer is heard (*ibid*, p. 40)

The Policy Response

For many years voluntary and philanthropic agencies such as Simon Communities of Ireland, Focus Ireland and Trust and the Campaign for the Homeless, as well as the Society of St. Vincent de Paul in more recent years, played leading roles in campaigning for the homeless and providing shelter on a temporary basis. Legislation and policy departures are relatively recent. These have taken a reasonably broad view, although this has only come after many years of campaigning on the ground. Indeed, until the Housing Act, 1988, the problem was hardly officially recognised at all. Nevertheless, Section 2 of the Act provided a fairly comprehensive interpretation of the problem[3]:

> A person shall be regarded by a housing authority as being homeless for the purposes of this Act if—
> (a) there is no accommodation available which, in the opinion of the authority, he, together with any other person who normally resides with him or who might reasonably be expected to reside with him, can reasonably occupy or remain in occupation of, or
> (b) he is living in a hospital, county home, night shelter or other such institution, and is so living because he has no accommodation of the kind referred to in paragraph (a), and he is, in the opinion of the authority, unable to provide accommodation from his own resources.

The Child Care Act 1991 was a further advance, obliging the Health Boards to provide care and accommodation for homeless children. The Homeless Initiative was established on 21 October 1996 by the then Minister for Housing and Urban Renewal, Liz McManus, with the broad aim of improving the breadth and coordination of service provision for homeless people in the Dublin Region. The publication of *Homelessness: An Integrated Strategy* (Government of Ireland, 2000b) brought significant progress and explicit recognition of the complexity and the multi-dimensional nature of the problem and the need for an equally comprehensive policy approach. Produced by a cross-departmental team, this government document formulated a broad strategy for dealing with homelessness covering accommodation, health, welfare, education and prevention. It called for "an integrated response to the many issues which affect homeless people, including emergency, institutional and long-term responses as well as issues relating to health, education, employment and home-making" (Government of Ireland, 2000b). The most immediate practical effect was the requirement that local authorities, health boards and voluntary agencies work in partnership (within Homeless Fora) to produce action plans at county level every three years to ensure all the relevant agencies provide an integrated response to homelessness.

Homelessness: An Integrated Strategy also acknowledged the special case of Dublin, where homelessness is particularly extensive and in many cases acute, and as a result the establishment of a special agency to oversee the implementation of the *Dublin Action Plan* was recommended. The Homeless Agency was thus set up in 2001, subsuming the functions of the earlier Homeless Initiative. The Agency rightly has as its ultimate target the elimination of homelessness in the capital by 2010 – in other words to negate the reason for its own existence (presumably the aim of any governmental or non-governmental organisation in the homeless field should similarly be to solve the problem and therefore disappear). The Agency is responsible for coordinating and managing responses to homelessness, and it operates a partnership structure with involvement of the key voluntary and statutory agencies with responsibility for responding to homelessness. Its work includes drawing up and implementing action plans, providing training, support and information, administering funding to services, and undertaking research on the nature of the problem and into best-practice responses.

The combined effect of these various initiatives has been to greatly improve and diversify homelessness responses in urban areas, particularly central Dublin. One approach has been to increase the use of B&B accommodation, which provides people with emergency accommodation from a private landlord. Voluntary agencies have also started to provide services for wider categories of homeless people (including low threshold hostels, "wet" hostels and youth accommodation). Threshold is now providing assistance for homeless people to acquire private rental accommodation through its Access Housing Unit (funded by the Homeless Agency), which helped 127 people out of emergency accommodation and into the private rental sector in 2004.

Thus, there has been progress, but there are still many policy challenges. The fragmentation of services remains a long-term concern regarding the efficacy of the response to homelessness (although the Homeless Agency has helped to make some progress in the case of Dublin, as have the creation of Homeless Fora throughout the country). There is a division of responsibility between several statutory agencies. The difficulties faced by a homeless child, for example, may variously be the responsibility of the Departments of Health, Education and Justice, while once a person turns eighteen years of age, responsibility for their accommodation shifts from the Health Board to the Local Authority. The result is that Health Boards often struggle to meet their responsibilities under the Child Care Act, and "solutions" reached are often questionable. For example, a former Director of Trinity House, a detention centre for children under sixteen years of age, stated that one third of those detained there were in fact homeless children who should not be there (McVerry, 1999). Despite the expansion in emergency beds, accessing such accommodation is not always straightforward. Most shelters are run by religious or voluntary groups, and they all have their own target groups and regulations (for example, some accept only teenagers or only adults; others require people to be drug-free and dry, others are "low threshold"). This can create difficulties for people on the street trying to work out where they can go, and for social workers trying to place young people. The continuing use of dormitory accommodation for emergency shelter is problematic and can be off-putting, even unsafe, particularly for more vulnerable people. Finally, the use of B&B accommodation, while providing a flexible response, comes at a considerable public cost. Annual expenditure nationally currently runs to about €20 million. This is a questionable use of resources and a considerable public support for private landlords in place of direct investment in long-term supported accommodation.

Although *Homelessness: An Integrated Strategy* has encouraged sectoral coordination and explicit plans, a review of the first round of plans carried out by four voluntary agencies (Focus Ireland, Simon Communities of Ireland, St. Vincent de Paul and Threshold) raised important concerns. First, there is no statutory basis for the strategy, and as a result many local authorities failed to produce their action plans on time. Second, *Homelessness: An Integrated Strategy* did not set specific targets for the reduction or elimination of homelessness, and outside of Dublin, the action plans are either silent or vague as to what the specific, practical aim of the exercise is. Third, it is not clear that appropriate resources are available to implement the aims of the various plans. Fourth, while there is more emergency accommodation available in hostels and B&Bs, strategies for prevention and for moving out of homelessness into stable, long-term accommodation are given less attention. Homelessness and its prevention are complex challenges and the interconnected problems of access across the tenures need to be addressed to reduce the incidence of homelessness and to improve pathways out of homelessness into sustainable accommodation. Thus, much remains to be done if homelessness in Dublin and elsewhere is indeed to be eliminated by 2010.

THE TRAVELLING COMMUNITY

There is little doubt that Travellers represent one of the most marginalised groups in Irish society. This reality is particularly obvious in the case of housing. The most recent Census of Population (CSO, 2004) recorded a total of 4,396 Traveller households, and a total population of 23,681. However, the most recent (2003) *Annual Count of Travellers* identified 6,799 Traveller families. The 2002 Census also showed that 1,655 households were in what was termed "temporary housing units". This was slightly higher than the 1,583 families assessed as in "housing need" in the 2002 Assessment of Needs. This means that between 36 and 38 per cent of Traveller families require more appropriate housing. Moreover, in view of the 2003 Annual Count, it may well be that this underestimates the extent of need. This problem is not a new one. Prior to the 1960s, the state paid very little attention to the accommodation needs of Travellers. At that time, very few had been allocated a home by the local authorities, and the vast majority lived a transient existence on the side of the road in caravans and without proper sanitary or other facilities. It must of course be acknowledged that many Travellers did not at that time seek local authority housing, as living in a settled community could conflict with their nomadic lifestyle and culture. In any case, the allocation of housing to Travellers was likely, for a variety of reasons, to meet with considerable opposition from most settled communities determined to prevent integration of this group. Furthermore, few attempts were made to provide even halting sites or basic facilities to enable Travellers to retain their lifestyles and cultural identity.

The first major government report – *The Commission on Itinerancy* (1963) – acknowledged the need for action. The main thrust of that report was a policy of "assimilation" or "integration" of Travellers into the settled community. However, it seems that the attempts to implement the recommendations were in effect "isolationist", since the halting sites provided by local authorities were in fact well removed from settled residential areas. Furthermore, the halting sites were detached from schools and social services – vital prerequisites for assimilation. The rules and regulations associated with halting sites also militated against maintaining family connections and traditional economic activities (Brady, 2000; Joyce, 2000).

Two decades later, little progress had been made and after a detailed study, the Economic and Social Research Institute concluded in 1986 that "the living conditions of Travellers are intolerable" and "no humane and decent society made aware of Travellers' living conditions could permit them to persist" (ESRI, 1986).

Ten years later the publication of the *Task Force on the Travelling Community* (Government of Ireland, 1995) marked an important change of attitude. For the first time, Travellers' representatives were involved in and played a key role in developing the Task Force recommendations. The Report could fairly be described as inclusive and respectful of the culture, traditions and nomadic heritage of the Travelling community. The then President of Ireland, Mary Robinson, put it as follows:

> When we talk about the Travelling Community it's not just a question of whether they want housing or whether they would prefer serviced halting sites. It's that they want their culture recognised, they want their dignity respected, they want to be full citizens of this country. I think that is the most important thing – that there is real space for the Travelling community, for their own culture, for their own self-development and self-expression; that we have space for them and that we value them; and then other things, like the appropriate kind of houses, services and facilities are provided to the best ability of the nation (Government of Ireland, 1995, p. 74).

Following publication of the Task Force Report the Department of the Environment produced a National Traveller Accommodation Strategy in March 1996 which proposed:

- Legislation on Traveller accommodation
- The establishment of a special unit within the Department of Environment and Local Government to co-ordinate an accommodation programme
- The establishment of a National Traveller Accommodation Consultative Group to advise the Minister
- The establishment of a National Traveller Accommodation Agency

To oversee this strategy a dedicated Traveller Accommodation Unit was established in the Department of the Environment and Local Government in May 1996. A National Accommodation Consultative Group was also established under the aegis of the Department in December 1996 and was later established on a statutory basis in April 1999. Arising from the *Report of the Task Force*, the Housing (Traveller Accommodation) Act was enacted in 1998. It required local authorities to prepare and adapt, in full consultation with Travellers, five-year programmes for Traveller accommodation to meet both existing and projected needs and required them to make all reasonable efforts in accordance with resources to implement these programmes within a reasonable time frame.

It should be noted that the obligation is to provide a permanent halting site rather than conventional dwellings. As happens with any planning proposal, the provision of such sites can of course meet with strong opposition, and this remains a considerable issue, as proposed sites are often successfully resisted by reference to zoning objectives or other planning grounds. The Task Force on the Travelling Community in 1995 had recommended the provision of

3,100 units of accommodation (1,200 permanent halting sites, 1,000 transient halting sites [bays] and 900 houses) by the year 2000. Provision over the eight-year period 1996 to 2003 is given in Table 5.8.

Table 5.8 Traveller Families in Local Authority Assisted Accommodation, 1996-2003

Type	1996	1999	2003	Change 1996-99	Change 1999-2003
Standard housing*	1,703	1,999	2,680	296	681
Group housing	301	356	545	55	189
Halting sites	1,063	1,100	1,398	37	298
Private houses**	N/A	128	329	128	201
Total	3,067	3,583	4,952	516	1,369

* Including voluntary
** Assisted by local authorities

Source: *Report of the Traveller Accommodation Consultative Committee, 2004*

It is clear that over the first four-year period, progress was very slow and only 516 of the 3,100 units were gained. A significant improvement took place in the period up to 2003, when a net gain of 1,369 units was achieved. However, this is still far short of requirements. Furthermore, in 2003 a total of 788 families (12 per cent of the total) were on unauthorised sites without proper washing or sanitary facilities.

The Department of the Environment and Local Government provides 100 per cent capital funding for the provision of new and redeveloped halting sites and group housing schemes for Travellers. Expenditure for such provision increased from €8.3 million in 1996 to €15.2 million in 2000 and between 2000 and 2003 a total of €94 million was allocated for Traveller accommodation (Department of the Environment Press Release, 19 January 2005, www. irl.gov.ie). However, no local authority has managed to meet its target over the period 2000 to 2003 and only about one third of the planned accommodation was provided. In 2004 an allocation of €40 million was made for Traveller accommodation – an increase of 33 per cent on the 2003 figure.

In a *Review of the Operation of the Housing (Traveller Accommodation) Act, 1998,* the National Traveller Accommodation Consultative Committee identified a number of barriers to implementing the accommodation programmes required under the Act. These included the difficulty in securing land at an affordable price and the absence of an absolute requirement (in Section 16 of the Act) on local authorities to implement programmes (National Traveller Accommodation Consultative Committee, 2004). This again points to the case for a right to housing for all citizens. There is no doubt that, even if the legislation were strengthened, local opposition to Traveller accommodation from the settled community would represent a continuing obstacle to progress.

HOUSING FOR PEOPLE WITH DISABILITIES

> People with disabilities are the neglected citizens of Ireland...Whether their status is looked at in terms of economics, information, education, mobility or housing they are seen to be treated as second class citizens.

Almost ten years ago, this was the introductory statement in the *Report of the Commission on the Status of People with Disabilities* (1996). The Commission concluded that by the mid 1990s there had been no tradition of local authorities providing "special housing" for people with disabilities, apart from housing for the elderly. Any special housing provision tended to be the initiative of the voluntary and co-operative housing sector. Neither was there a policy of providing "lifetime adaptable homes" or of providing a quota of wheelchair accessible housing. The Commission's Working Group referred to the "appalling lack of public statistics on either the housing situation or the housing requirements of people with disabilities" (Commission on the Status of People with Disabilities, 1995). The Commission made twenty three recommendations for change, including the adoption of a policy of Lifetime Adaptable Housing entailing an improvement in Building Regulations, the collection of a whole range of statistics, detailed assessments of current residential centres, as well as a Charter of Rights for residents and the removal of people with disabilities inappropriately placed in institutions such as psychiatric hospitals. In a *Progress Report* in 1999 on the implementation of the Commission recommendations, it was reported that the Building Regulations would be amended, that new statistical data on the needs of people with disabilities would be collected and that various recommendations were being "implemented on an ongoing basis" (Government of Ireland, 1999b). No progress report was produced since that time.

The Building Regulations were amended in 2000, requiring that all new public and private buildings after 2001 be "accessible" to people with disabilities. However, there is evidence that developers are not always complying with the new Regulations and that local authorities are carrying out insufficient inspections to ensure compliance (*Irish Examiner*, 11 September 2004).

Unfortunately, the statistical data relating to the housing requirements of many categories of disability remains unsatisfactory. However, the Health Research Board has been compiling a very useful annual *National Intellectual Disability Database* since 1996, and it is possible to compare this data with the first *Census of Mental Handicap* in 1974. In

2005, 24,917 people were registered on this database (Barron and Mulvany, 2005). The data illustrates that the proportion of people with moderate, severe or profound intellectual disability over 35 years of age has increased from 29 per cent of the total in 1974 to 47 per cent in 2005. This reflects the increase in the lifespan of people with intellectual disability. This has major implications for service planning, including the ongoing need for full-time residential services and residential support services.

Table 5.9 shows that the vast majority (15,827 or 64 per cent of the total) of those with intellectual disabilities reside at home either with parents or relatives. A total of 8,073 are accommodated in full-time residential services, mainly in group homes and residential centres, but 396 people were still inappropriately accommodated in psychiatric hospitals and a further 55 in mental health community residences (Barron and Mulvany, 2005, p. 39). Table 5.9 also shows that the main source of accommodation is now group homes with the numbers in residential and other services falling since 1996. The net gain in places over the ten-year period is only 501 or 50 places per annum. Over 3,000 of those currently living at home are in the older age categories (35 years or more) and are thus likely to have elderly parents. This underlines the need for full-time residential services mentioned above. The requirement over the last three years alone has increased by 23 per cent, and it is estimated that a further 2,008 residential places will be required over the period 2006-2010 – the highest since the database was established in 1996 (Barron and Mulvany, 2005, p. 64). In other words, the annual requirement (500 per annum) over the next four years is ten times greater than that achieved in the past.

Table 5.9　Main Residential Circumstances of People with Intellectual Disabilities, 1996-2005

	1996		2005	
	Number	%	Number	%
At home with parents or relative	16,267	60.9	15,827	63.5
Independent living	526	2.0	810	3.3
Total Residential Places	**7,572**	**28.4**	**8,073**	**32.4**
Community group home	2,393	9.0	3,502	14.0
Residential Centre	3,824	14.3	3,334	13.4
Other full-time services	1,355	5.1	1,237	5.0
Of which psychiatric hospitals	(970)	(3.6)	(396)	(1.6)
No fixed abode	6	0.02	9	0.03
Insufficient information	2,323	8.7	198	0.8
TOTAL	26,694	100.0	24,917	100.0

Source: *National Intellectual Disability Database*, 1996 and 2005

THE PROBLEM OF SEGREGATION

Over the years many Local Authorities have, perhaps unwittingly, pursued a policy of "segregation" by concentrating low-income families in particular geographical areas. As an example, considerable numbers have been relocated from the inner city of Dublin to the periphery of the city where some estates contained up to 90 per cent Local Authority tenants. The same holds for cities such as Cork, Limerick and Galway and many other smaller towns throughout the country. At the same time, very little residential building by Local Authorities took place in the central area or "inner cities". The "surrender grant" of the 1980s had the adverse effect of denuding some Local Authority estates of those who were employed on relatively high incomes and their replacement with further low-income families, thus contributing further to a sense of residualisation.

The placing of "problem tenants" in particular flat complexes or estates further exacerbated the problem. The end result – still with us today – is a concentration of low-income families in a poor physical environment with high levels of unemployment, educational disadvantage and a range of social problems, including drug abuse. This has led to the regrettable and erroneous impression that to live in Local Authority housing is somehow to have failed. Furthermore, the segregation of low-income households into "Local Authority" housing may be worsening, as evidenced by Household Budget figures, which show a steady "residualisation" of the sector in terms of the relative income levels of tenants (Table 5.10). This is reflected in the levels of poverty experienced among local authority households. The case of Dublin makes this point clear (Table 5.11).

Table 5.10 Index of average disposable income by household tenure in Ireland, 1973-2000

Year	Owned outright	Mortgaged	Private rental	Local authority rental	Rent free	State
1973	100.6	119.8	83.1	85.7	61.6	100.0
1980	91.6	126.1	87.4	73.4	69.1	100.0
1987	91.0	127.6	91.8	64.6	68.5	100.0
1994-95	88.2	129.7	87.1	57.0	84.5	100.0
1999-2000	87.1	127.5	101.2	55.6	83.1	100.0

Source: *Household Budget Survey*, various years

It is important to appreciate that segregation of this kind is not necessarily *inherent* to social housing and must be understood in its broader context. In part this problem is a wholly

Table 5.11 Poverty among Dublin City Council Tenant
Households compared to general Irish population

	DCC Tenants (2001)	Ireland (1998)
% less than 40% of average income	39.2	9.1
% less than 50% of average income	62.5	20.4
% less than 60% of average income	73.1	27.2

Source: Murray and Norris, 2002

predictable outcome of the policies that have residualised
social housing – it is the reduction of this tenure to a welfare
role and the restriction of access to the most marginalised
families that led to the concentration of low-income households and the stigmatisation of the entire tenure. It is also
apparent that segregation and inequality are integral elements in market-driven housing systems. Those from the
lower social classes are excluded or displaced from the highly valued areas through the prohibitive cost of housing, rapidly escalating land prices and the lack of non-market
options. These élite residential areas are thereby ring-fenced
from the poor or other "undesirable" social groups on the
grounds that they might "downgrade" the area or adversely
affect house prices. In effect, this distinction between highly
valued "good" areas and stigmatised "bad" areas underpins
the price differentials that are evident across the housing
market. In this market model, access and housing choice
depend on ability to pay. As a result, the poorest groups have
the least choice and end up in the least desirable locations,
while the richest can access the more exclusive areas, where
property prices are highest to begin with, and there is strong
expectation of steady future increases. This duality begs the
question as to whether inequality and segregation to some
extent prop up the housing property market – what are the

socio-economic relations between the segregated £1 million-per-house enclave and the inner city ghetto or the peripheral deprived urban neighbourhood?

A representative of the Irish Auctioneers and Valuers Institute put the case for segregation (in opposition to policies to promote tenure integration):

> In future, people will speak of pre and post 1999 developments ... whether they live in mixed developments or are among the lucky few residing in segregated private schemes. Of course, we don't approve of such snobbish attitudes – publicly. Privately, however, most of us will continue to do what we have always done – pay considerably more to be among the latter group (*Irish Times*, 14 October, 1999).

In response to a number of critical social concerns in Irish housing, Part V of the Planning and Development Act (Government of Ireland, 2000a) introduced a number of policy departures. The stated aim of this legislation was to provide for the future housing requirements of the population and to avoid "undue segregation". The most important change in planning practice was the requirement that each local authority should produce a "housing strategy" as part of its periodic *Development Plan*. The change that received most attention, however, was the stipulation that the authority could require the provision of up to 20 per cent of any residential development for "social and affordable housing" as a condition of planning permission. The underlying aims were not just to assuage the problems facing many low- and mid-income households in the booming housing market, but also to reduce segregation, ensure some planning gain for the community and calm down the rate of increase in development land prices.

It may be noted that this was, in fact, a market-oriented mechanism, insofar as it depended largely on the co-operation and actions of private developers to provide or facilitate social and affordable housing. This meant that, rather than direct provision by the Local Authority, the provision of social and affordable housing remains dependent on reaching agreement with private developers, leaving little public control over location, phasing, design or quality. In any case, very few houses were constructed under the Act since sectional interests in the building industry opposed the integration measures, a campaign that met with quick success. Under pressure, the provisions were significantly diluted by the Minister for the Environment and Local Government in late 2002, before the new planning practice had adequate time to 'bed in'. In particular the construction sector and related interests were strongly and vocally opposed to the social integration measures, arguing against the transfer of units within a development in particular, and a related 'withering rule', whereby existing planning permissions were to lapse within two years – a measure intended under the Act to make sure that the new system got up and running as soon as possible.

The critical change in response to these pressures was to remove the "withering rule" and to dilute the 20 per cent social and affordable provision. In particular, under the original Part V, the local authority could negotiate as a condition of planning permission the transfer of land, transfer of sites or transfer of completed units. Under the 'new' Part V, the 'deal' could involve these same three transfers within the proposed development or the transfer of land elsewhere, sites elsewhere, a cash option or all of the above.

The intent of the Act to deal with social segregation and the effort to ensure some degree of community gain (in the shape of social and affordable housing, acquired at below "market" value) were welcome. Indeed, the central premise of the Act is that it is indeed possible to acquire land for development at existing use-value – a provision that withstood a constitutional challenge on the grounds of social justice and the common good.

However, we might look again at the renewed emphasis on "area-based' solutions, inherent to the Act, which focuses in a special way on the need to "avoid undue segregation" (the phrase used in Part V of the Planning and Development Act, 2000, begs an intriguing question: that is, what degree of segregation is acceptable, and just when does the degree of segregation become excessive?). Once again, many seem to have taken this area-based policy as common sense – much as the classical urban sociologists looking at early 20th century Chicago, for whom the construction of socially and ethnically divided cities was a frightening dimension of modernity, a social time bomb. Experiences in Dublin with large, segregated public estates on the periphery seemed to bear this out.

Nevertheless, undue emphasis has arguably been placed on physical and spatial solutions to social problems which may be related to social class rather than simple location, in which case area-based policies can run into difficulty. The problem is that such policies are underpinned by a questionable spatial and environmental determinism. Certainly getting the location of residential development right and improving living environments will generate some positive benefits, but such changes are not sufficient responses in themselves in relation to the causes and social consequences of inequality and poverty – nor adequate responses to the complex problems that raise even broader structural issues about uneven development and power. There is much more at issue than housing or residential location.

On the surface, the inherent faith in social mixing seems to make common sense – there seems a de facto case for moving away from the creation of mass public-housing estates. The problem is that the negative outcomes of the past are not necessarily simply attributable to the location of any one single tenure. A complex range of factors must be looked at including the precise causes of social inequality and poverty as well as the provision (or lack of provision) of appropriate services, amenities, education, employment opportunities and other relevant requirements. By turning to tenure mixing alone as a solution, the Act places a lot of faith in the potential efficacy of social engineering in particular areas. It is difficult to say how effective this will in fact prove – certainly, the social effects will need careful monitoring.

In any event, the operation of Part V to date has been disappointing, producing only 75 social housing units (for rent) and 88 affordable ones (for sale at a discount) during 2003. Up to the end of 2004, a further 591 units had been produced. This policy might yet become more effectively embedded in the planning process, and a better return might be achieved in the next few years. The concern is, that if the performance has been slow during years of record levels of production, what will happen when this boom slackens off or, indeed, during times of considerable downturn in property cycles?

Moreover, it was hardly surprising that an integration policy so heavily reliant on the co-operation of profit-driven private developers would have a modest impact. Such concerns are inevitably part and parcel of a housing paradigm that leans more and more on market-driven mechanisms to achieve social policy aims and which by its nature guarantees much uncertainty regarding the quantity, location, phasing and quality of the housing that may result.

CONCLUSIONS

A number of important conclusions and policy implications can be drawn from this chapter. The difficulties in either purchasing or renting a home at an affordable price means that the number of families and individuals in housing need has increased significantly over the last decade. As a result, we believe that the most recent official figures seriously under-estimate the extent of the problem. We estimate that 250,000 people may require housing but are not in a position to either purchase or rent at an affordable price. There is thus an urgent need for an expanded construction programme of public housing by all non-profit providers – including local authorities, housing associations, co-operatives and other voluntary and community development organisations. The current policy of selling off local authority housing at a huge discount also needs to be reviewed as a matter of urgency. Finally, there is a strong case for broadening the base of public housing provision as has happened in other European countries in order to give it the status it deserves. This would involve a new role for public/social housing in providing "general needs" housing for the middle classes who cannot afford the current house prices as well as for its traditional clients. The financial surplus generated from renting to middle-income residents could cross-subsidise the costs of providing housing for poorer households. This could also help to address the problems of segregation, stigmatisation and residualisation.

Notes

1. Total social housing stock comprises about 16,000 voluntary and co-operative and 109,000 Local Authority units (NESC, 2004, p. 64). Since 88,200 of the latter units were occupied (Table1.2), it suggests a vacancy level of 20,800 or 19 per cent.
2. Many homeless people are not on local authority waiting lists. In particular, single-person households, who make up a majority of the homeless population, do not easily access such lists.
2 It should be noted, however, that the definition in the Act leaves considerable ambiguities allowing people to widen or narrow the definition of homelessness depending on their perspectives and/or the individual that presents (Bergin et al. 2005). This has obvious practical implications in terms of the provision of homeless services, the interpretation and implementation of policies, and research.

Chapter 6

Privatising Public Housing: Social Progress or Selling the City?

I t is the contention of this book that the balance of priorities in housing policy – between home or commodity – has taken a turn towards a market ideology that manifests itself in numerous ways. In a broad sense, this can be traced through the relative emphasis on economic as against social priorities in policymaking, and in the urban context this is arguably evident in the adoption by the local authority of an increasingly flexible role as an enabler of market forces. This is in contrast to a traditional philosophy, which emphasised in the main local government's redistributive role as a public housing authority or regulatory role as a planning authority. In Dublin, this process is perhaps at its most advanced, underpinning a substantial realignment of urban planning and housing policy over a number of years. This has had its practical expression in such approaches as the use of tax incentive schemes to attract private development capital, the creation of special-interest agencies to promote the redevelopment (and "re-packaging" and marketing) of defined areas for high-class users and a de-prioritisation of direct intervention in the city through public housing construction.

Market ideologies are now seeping right down into very local public housing areas, as revealed, for instance, through recent housing strategies and urban regeneration plans, currently at various stages of implementation or being proposed for the future. In this chapter we examine some examples of these, most notably the recent vogue for public-private partnerships (PPPs) in local housing policy, as well as the application of Part V measures and the sale of public housing and land (See also O'Toole, 2003 and Sweeney, 2004 for a critical analysis of other privatisation experiments). These are interesting analytically as "live" examples of an emerging market shift in the housing system, but they are also of critical importance both because of the immediate implications for current tenants and the longer-term consequences for the public housing system and poorer households in general. That this is happening in Dublin City is particularly noteworthy since 22 per cent of the state's entire publicly rented stock is within this local authority area. What happens here will have a disproportionate effect on the nature of the Irish public-housing system.

SELLING OFF PUBLIC LAND

Although one of the major problems faced by the local authority in meeting housing need in Dublin is the high cost of land, paradoxically, the city has been highly active in the sale of land to the private sector for commercial use. The case of Sheriff Street in Dublin's docklands was an important early example. This was a locality that endured many decades of physical and social decline due to the corrosive effects of job loss in the docks, unemployment, poverty, educational disadvantage, and the heroin crisis. It was also arguably faced with the slow erosion of community spirit through an apparent policy of using the flats complex as a "sink" for problem tenants. By the time the adjacent Customs House Docks Development scheme with its centerpiece, the new International Financial Services Centre, came on track in the late 1980s, Sheriff Street was therefore struggling with a range of complex problems – social, economic, health. It soon became apparent that, with the advent of Docklands renewal policies, the value and the future of the Sheriff Street site was being rapidly reassessed by both local authority and private developers. Locally, awareness of forthcoming plans came first in 1989 when the then Minister for the Environment, Pádraig Flynn, issued a directive that the flats were to be detenanted and demolished. Community bulletins were circulated at this time to build consciousness, and these capture the mood locally:

> It is now little over a year ago since Patrick Flynn announced what was and is in effect a death sentence on the Sheriff Street community. This directive, if implemented, would not alone see the demolition and scattering of the people, it would also have a knock-on effect for the whole community. For instance, it would almost certainly herald the immediate closure of two of our local schools and in due course all of our schools. It would be the thin end of the wedge for the eventual takeover of all our community. There is now little doubt that this was the real objective, the people and the community were seen as expendable – as surplus to requirements (North Wall Community Association, 1990).

The plans were resisted based on one simple conviction: "the rights of a Community should never be regarded as subordinate to those of commercial interest. A proper housing policy is central to the success of Inner City renewal and regeneration" (North Wall Community Association, 1993). Eventually, a compromise was reluctantly reached whereby the remaining tenants[1] would be rehoused locally by the local authority, while the flats would be demolished and most of the older Sheriff Street site redeveloped by selling it off to a private developer. Accordingly, the local authority built 113 units along the northern strip of the site, and detenanted the old flats in the mid-1990s, selling off the rest of the site (10 acres) to Chesterbridge Developments Ltd in 1994 for £2.4 million. This was duly redeveloped for private residential use in the main (580 apartments in 5- and 6-storey blocks), as well as some commercial units, and renamed "Custom House Square". This became a gated and segregated development (including razor wire at one point), separated off from the new public housing behind it. A considerable number of these new apartments were sold to investors, including staff from at least one estate agency. A walk down Commons Street brings one through an odd and telling situation, past the gates and the razor wire and, on the left, the infamous towering wall that hems in the new Custom House Docks apartments from the older Dublin streets outside. The environment changes abruptly from urban penthouse and loft living to Sheriff Youth Club and the new public housing area, two very different social spaces, side by side, worlds apart. The Sheriff Street "model" was a particularly extreme example, but the policy of privatising the public land bank continued apace through the 1990s, such that by 1998, 78 tracts of public land had been privately redeveloped (McGuirk and MacLaran, 2001). Thus, as well as various tax incentive schemes, local authority land policy became a major driver of the private redevelopment of the city, with predictable gains for investors and speculators but little to offer for poorer residents increasingly priced out of the historic urban core.

PART V AND THE LOCAL HOUSING STRATEGY

The introduction of Part V of the Planning and

Development Act (2000) and its subsequent amendment (2002) provided an important central-government impetus for housing–policy change, as noted earlier. The Act made housing a material consideration of planning, in that it was now a requirement for local authorities to produce a housing strategy as part of their development plans. This was to analyse and plan for housing need and provision, including social and "affordable" needs, residential land, integration and sustainable development. This included a policy whereby up to 20 per cent of new residential developments could be acquired by the local authority for the purposes of social (for rent from the local authority or housing association) and "affordable" (for sale at a subsidised price for private ownership) housing, where such a need was identified. This mechanism was also seen as a means of avoiding "undue" social segregation (in practice, by introducing a policy of tenure mixing). However, the different interpretations and implementations of these general provisions at local level is an important consideration. In the Dublin City context, the first housing strategy in 2001 identified significant housing need (the strategy recorded an existing waiting list of 7,530 households, while it was estimated that 36 per cent of all new households would not be able to afford to purchase homes). Accordingly, the council's strategy required the full 20 per cent social and affordable in new developments, and this was to be split between social and affordable units (10 per cent of each).

However, the housing strategy also included a policy of not providing additional social housing where a concentration already existed in order to achieve a "better" social mix. In effect, it was decided that in wards where public housing already exceeded 50 per cent of total housing, the 10 per cent social provision would not apply, thus disqualifying 22 wards (clustered in the north-east and south west inner city, along with Cherry Orchard, Ballymun and Priorswood) from additional public housing. The practical difficulty was that these areas housed populations on low incomes and with a considerable need for publicly rented housing; yet no new local authority units were permitted under the 2001 housing strategy. At the same time, of course, many of these inner-city wards saw a flood of high-cost private development of little local benefit. In short, in the interests of "social mixing", a major effect of the policy was to promote middle class colonisation of working-class areas (legitimising gentrification, in effect). At the very least, the commitment to social mixing would be more convincing if there was an equally robust strategy for introducing social housing to the vast, one-class, single-tenure, segregated housing estates of Dublin 4 and elsewhere. In any event, a combination of factors, including this social mixing policy and the flexible arrangements introduced under the 2002 amendment to the Planning Act, has meant that only two units of social housing had been acquired under Part V in Dublin City by the end of 2004 (Department of Environment, 2005). This fact sits uneasily with the Council's assumption that "the main source of social housing provision in the future is...likely to be by way of Part V agreements" (Kenny, 2004).

PUBLIC CONTROL AND MASTER PLANNING

The well-known case of Ballymun provides a far more ambitious approach to urban regeneration, with a major focus on public housing. Constructed between 1965 and 1969, Ballymun housed a population of over 16,500 people in just over 5,000 dwellings, in the main in high-rise public flats. This experiment, along classical Le Corbusier lines, was doomed to failure due to their unsuitability for families, inadequate maintenance, poor management, neglect and the broader complex problems of poverty and social deprivation. Following community consultation, the

Ballymun Regeneration Masterplan was released in 1998, promising a complete demolition of the tower blocks and the construction of what would essentially be a "new town" in the north suburbs. The other aims of the regeneration programme included the replacement of the towers with houses and low-rise flats, increasing job access, improving education and training, promoting a strong and positive neighbourhood identity and rejuvenating the town centre (Muir, 2004). The envisaged timeframe was 1998-2012 or later, and the project was managed by Ballymun Regeneration Ltd., a private company wholly owned by Dublin City Council with an appointed board. Participation was facilitated through five estate forums involving elected residents as well as public officials. By 2004, the programme was about 60 per cent complete (Muir, 2005). This constitutes an important effort at publicly-led master planning and regeneration, although it must be said that in many ways, it is also something of a unique case, given the scale of the undertaking and the challenges involved. It is much too early to form a judgement on the success or otherwise of this scheme in terms of participation, community development, amenity provision, sustainability, social cohesion, the quality of the built environment and other central concerns.

PUBLIC PRIVATE PARTNERSHIPS

The most radical change now being implemented on the ground – with potentially enormous implications for the future of public housing in the city – is the adoption of public-private partnership (PPP) models for regeneration. This is in line with the recent vogue for PPPs that has infused many areas of government policy, though not without controversy. Notably, for example, the National Development Plan (NDP) 2000-2006 envisaged a move towards PPPs as vehicles to deliver economic and social infrastructure, though the emphasis was on roads, water, public transport and waste management projects rather than on housing. The *Programme for Prosperity and Fairness* (2000) also noted that PPPs would make a very significant contribution to the implementation of the infrastructural projects identified under the NDP. A Central Public Private Partnerships Unit was established in the Department of Finance to "lead, drive and coordinate the PPP process" (http://www.ppp.gov.ie/about/index html). The main function of this unit is to develop the legislative framework, provide technical and policy guidance and disseminate best practices. The legislative framework was set out in the State Authorities (Public Private Partnerships Arrangements) Act (2002), which enabled State Authorities to enter into PPPs, including joint ventures, while the National Development Finance Agency Act (2002) provided for the creation of the National Development Finance Agency (NDFA) to assist in providing effective project financing. The official enthusiasm for PPPs was confirmed in the more recent *Sustaining Progress: Social Partnership Agreement, 2003-05*. Finally, in July 2005, the Minister for Finance announced the creation of a single, specialised "Centre of Expertise" (Located in the NDFA) with responsibility for the procurement of all new PPP projects in Central Government.

The immediate impetus for the use of PPPs in local authority housing was a circular from the Department of the Environment:

> Local authorities should consider the extent to which additional housing supply can be brought on stream through PPPs between local authorities and private developers utilising suitable local authority lands.
>
> These lands would primarily be lands in areas where there is already a significant concentration of social housing and where the total development of available sites for social housing would not be appropriate having regard to

the need to secure a suitable social mix in the area or due to the size of the site.

In deciding on whether to use some of their land bank on this type of initiative, the local authority should ensure that sufficient lands are reserved for their multi-annual LA housing programme
(Department of the Environment, Circular HS 13/01, 2001).

This approach has been taken on with enthusiasm by Dublin City Council more so than in any other authority to date. As of June 2005, there were seven PPP projects involving housing in process at various stages, five of which are in Dublin. These are demolition/regeneration projects at Fatima Mansions (currently under construction), St. Michael's Estate (under local consultation) and O'Devaney Gardens (a "selected bidder" from a shortlist of five tenders is about to be announced at time of writing), as well as affordable housing initiatives at Jamestown Road and Infirmary Road. These latter two are also developments on public land (owned by the Office of Public Works). Outside Dublin, PPP harbour redevelopment projects (including an element of housing) are in progress at Bray and Greystones (a shortlist of tenders is under appraisal in both cases).

The first PPP regeneration project at Fatima Mansions is just a beginning it would seem, as Dublin City Council has made it clear that it is going to target many other flats complexes across the city for similar PPP demolition/redevelopment projects, in the process affecting a dramatic transformation of the social and physical fabric.

Fatima Mansions and St. Michael's Estate
These are two public housing flats complexes in central Dublin constructed, respectively, between 1949-1951 and in the early 1970s. Fatima was built on an 11-acre site and consisted of 394 flats, while St. Michael's Estate was built on 14 acres at Keogh Square in Inchicore, consisting of 346 flats.

These developments housed vibrant communities for a number of decades, forming a small part of the complex social fabric of the inner city with close organic links to the industrial economic functions of the immediate area. People in both communities were proud of their localities and many strands of grassroots activism emerged creating dense kinship networks of reciprocal activity and co-operation (Kelleher and Whelan, 1992).

As with Sheriff Street and other localities, a combination of global processes and state policies created new and unexpected pressures, and a spiral of decay set in from the 1980s onwards. The destructive impacts of economic restructuring had a pronounced effect, as local industries either closed or relocated and unemployment grew rapidly. Tragically and with sudden ferocity, the heroin crisis also took root in the early 1980s amid general conditions of social dereliction, urban decay and policy neglect. The situation was compounded by housing policies, including poor allocation practices and the ill-conceived "surrender-grant" of the mid-1980s, which offered a cash bonus (IR£5,000) to tenants who relocated to private housing, giving up an existing local authority tenancy. Communities such as Fatima and St. Michael's almost did surrender, being faced with an out-flux of tenants in employment, many of whom were active leaders in their community, to be replaced by more marginalised people, sometimes with complex social difficulties (Fatima Groups United, 2000; St. Michael's Estate Regeneration Team, 2002).

The result was that these two areas for many years epitomised the inner-city crisis, being beset by a range of complex social problems. With the help of some elements of the media that tended to look for the sensational (the drug lords, the crime) and ignore the full story of struggle and community resilience, these localities became seen as veritable "no-go area" associated only with a decayed living environment, problem drug use, mass unemployment and low incomes. The population also declined as these multiple problems intensified and many households transferred out. This is a critical part of the cycle, since the de-tenanting of communities is a process that undermines social cohesion, reduces local leadership and grassroots power, and hastens physical decay (as flats remain empty and fall into disrepair). Crucially, at a much later date, this social decline provided an apparent legitimation for clean-sweep regeneration policies based on a complete remaking of the sites for, in the main, a new population.

Regeneration Plans

Clear policies for regeneration were only explored in a serious way since about 2000, beginning with community plans, leading into sometimes fraught processes of consultation, and eventually agreed Master Plans, until finally a different approach – demolition and redevelopment by PPP – (quite abruptly) became the local authority's preferred way forward. The full story behind these two PPP projects makes for an intriguing drama in itself, full of tensions, conflicts, peace talks, collapsed negotiations, street protest and last-minute political interventions. At this stage, however, it will only be possible to sketch the bare outlines, before raising some critical questions that deserve immediate consideration about the relevance of the PPP concept to real social, as well as physical, regeneration and the economic rationale and long-term viability of such approaches to the "proper planning and development" of public land.

In the context of considerable social disadvantage and state neglect, both communities mobilised at various junctures, generating a complex and vibrant grassroots infrastructure and a range of bottom-up responses aimed at improving the conditions of everyday life. Crucially in both cases this included the production of landmark community plans for regeneration. In the case of Fatima, *Eleven Acres, Ten Steps* (2000), outlined the principal aims of *social* as well as physical regeneration ("ten sensible steps to a flagship Fatima" – see Table 6.1), while also recommending key structures needed to move the regeneration process forward.

Table 6.1 Ten sensible steps to a Flagship Fatima

1. Secure an integrated regeneration programme for Fatima Mansions in the context of the wider Rialto neighbourhood
2. Retain the use of the existing 11 acre site for the provision of a choice of quality homes and community facilities for all residents of Fatima
3. Implement community-based estate management procedures
4. Facilitate the community to participate fully in the regeneration and sustainable development of Fatima
5. Maximise employment opportunities and develop the local social economy
6. Combat educational disadvantage and early school leaving
7. Optimise the potential of young people in Fatima
8. Tackle the high rates of ill-health and improve the holistic well-being and spirit of the community
9. Create a safe and secure neighbourhood for all to enjoy
10. Improve the quality of life in the whole neighbourhood of Rialto through recreational and cultural programmes

Source: Fatima Groups United (2000) *Eleven Acres, Ten Steps*

A similar document produced by the St. Michael's Estate Regeneration Team on behalf of the Blocks Committee, *Past, Present, Future,* also set out a clear vision:

> Our overall aim for the regeneration of St. Michael's Estate shall be one whereby the residents of the estate are treated with dignity and integrity and are guaranteed quality of life, quality housing, quality services, quality community

facilities and amenities within the newly regenerated estate (*Past, Present, Future: A Community Vision for the Regeneration of St. Michael's Estate, 2002*)

In this way, these two communities managed to "get ahead of the game" in terms of local organisational structures, knowledge and understanding, vision and action.[2] Consequent to these documents, intense negotiations with the city council began leading to the eventual agreement of Master Plans for the complete regeneration of both estates, driven by a programme of direct public investment. In Fatima, for example, Dublin City Council produced a draft Master Plan in 2001, subsequently revised to a final agreed plan after consultation. It was proposed at this stage to demolish the existing complex and replace it with an entirely new development comprising social, affordable and private housing. In total, approximately 220 homes were to be provided for social housing (a mix of traditional houses and apartments), while the private element was to consist of approximately 280 (Dublin City Council, *Regeneration/Next Generation* 2002). The proceeds of the sale of the land for private development were to fund community/sports facilities and other crucial requirements for social regeneration set out in the Master Plan. Importantly, consultation on and management of the regeneration was to be facilitated through a legally constituted structure with its own resources and an independent chair, the *Fatima Regeneration Board*, involving all stakeholders (see Figure 6.1).

Similarly in St. Michael's Estate, a lengthy process of negotiation was carried out through the St. Michael's Estate Task Force (involving tenants, residents from the wider area, Dublin City Council officials and councillors, community workers and statutory agencies) between 2001 and 2003. This resulted in an agreed plan based on the complete demolition of the existing flats and the development of 170 local authority houses, as well as some private (70) and affordable housing (80) units to introduce tenure mix on the estate. It also promised a series of measures for "social inclusion" and new and improved community facilities. There was much relief locally at this point, the process being compared to "signing off the Good Friday Agreement" (Fagan, 2004).

Figure 6.1 Fatima Regeneration Board: Membership and Issues

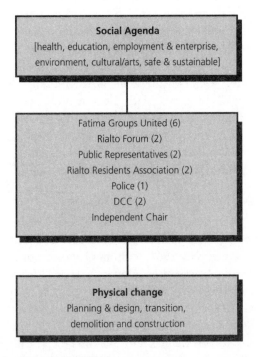

Source: Fatima Groups United (2004a)

At this time there was considerable hope in both communities that their estates were finally going to see a turnaround for the better, and relations between the city council and the local community, for long antagonistic, had improved notably and some level of trust had painstakingly been built up. In August 2003, the Fatima Regeneration Festival celebrated this new hope, as well as commemorating the many complex, contradictory and deeply felt attachments to the place held by local people. *The Fatima Wake* and *The Fatima Story* provided room to reflect and record the personal histories of a community with much spirit and solidarity, as well as the experiences of poverty, neglect and fear (Patrick Butler, *Irish Times,* August 11 2003).

In September 2003, however, it was announced that funding for the projects had been withdrawn by central government and that regeneration would instead be delivered through a public-private partnership. These announcements were completely unexpected at grassroots level and were greeted with considerable alarm and anger locally, as people came face to face with their own deepening disempowerment, devastated by the fact that the work of years of consultation could be so summarily abandoned. They were now entering into a new phase of uncertainty and a very different kind of planning and development process.

Regeneration by Public Private Partnership?

In Fatima Mansions, a Request for Qualifications (RFQ – see Box 6.1 for technical details) was released with a deadline of 13 September 2003, inviting proposals for a development of the 11 acre site in two phases. The subsequent Request for Proposals indicated that the first phase would comprise 110 social housing units (half the number agreed in the 2002 Master Plan) for which design documentation and exemption from planning permission already existed (these would re-house most of the remaining community). The second phase was to comprise private units in the main, along with 40 social and 70 affordable dwellings. Commercial facilities and a community/leisure centre were also to be included. Thus, the first major difference between the old and the new plans would be to dilute the social component from the 394 units originally constructed at Fatima in the 1950s down to 150 and to increase the private element significantly. Finally, a Preferred Bidder was selected in January 2004.

Note: The Request for Proposals for the Fatima project is advertised: eleven acres in Dublin 8 – a major mixed-use development opportunity – ready to go. The ad also lists some of the site's attractions, including its prime Dublin 8 location, the Digital Hub, St. James Hospital, and "its own Luas stop".

Box 6.1 PPPs in Housing: Planning and Tendering

The PPP process is complex, involving several stages leading to an agreement between the local authority and a selected private developer or development consortium. The key stages are as follows:

Request for qualifications (RFQ)
The local authority advertises the proposed development opportunity. Interested developers apply for the RFQ for a fee (€200 in the case of Fatima). The RFQ outlines the broad proposed development and invites expressions of interest and submissions of professional details relating to the criteria for qualification (including details on annual financial turnover).

Shortlisting
A short list of (usually) five developers is drawn up based on various criteria. One of the most interesting qualifications used in recent PPPs was that the developer had to show an average annual construction turnover of at least €75 million over the previous three years. This would indicate a preference for relatively large developers.

Request for Proposals (RFP)
This is a highly detailed tendering document, which amongst other issues sets out the features that must be provided by the developer – that is, the *legal burdens* which must be provided by the private partner. For example, this might include a specified number of social units to be returned to the state, community facilities and a defined percentage of open space. Apart from this, it is up to the developer to add non-specified features to the proposed plan, most importantly the commercial, profit-making elements (e.g. private housing units, commercial facilities, underground car parking, etc.). The RFP will also include development insurances and some indications as to the proposed role of the local authority (in particular, whether the speculative entrant to the deal is to bear all the costs or whether there will be some public investment).

Select Preferred Bidder
After a set deadline, the local authority examines the submitted out-line plans from the shortlisted developers, and an expert panel selects a "winning" bid according to defined criteria.

Sign PPP legal agreement
A contract is then signed by the local authority and the private developer to deliver the project jointly.

Local Authority applies directly to An Bórd Pleanála for Planning Permission
An important feature of this approach is that it bypasses standard local planning processes. The application must go through a routing known as Section 8 Modified. This requires the preparation of an Environmental Impact Statement (an EU requirement on certain projects likely to have a significant effect on the environment) and the whole application is lodged directly with An Bórd Pleanála. Unlike standard planning applications, the only routing for third-party objections is to make observations directly to An Bórd Pleanála. Crucially, the RFP will determine the grounds for planning objections.

The effect of this process is the formation of a "partnership" development project on land that was heretofore entirely publicly owned, within which the developer will provide an agreed number of public facilities (housing, community amenities) and a proportion of open or amenity space, while the rest of the site will be developed commercially for sale on the market. In effect, the cost to the developer of providing the public facilities and open space is offset by the "gift" of the rest of the site for commercial exploitation.

(**Source:** After Kelly and Punch, 2005)

Intense negotiations between the local authority and the community continued for a number of months under the auspices of the Fatima Regeneration Board (it was still the case, from the time of the earlier negotiations, that this Board had to sign off on the regeneration plan before a contract would be signed with the private consortium). Eventually, a deal was struck in May 2004, including the following main social regeneration policies:

- 150 social units in total (as set out in the RFP), Phase 1 (110) to be constructed immediately
- Allocation policies to deal with overcrowding
- Right-to-buy of the new social units – 30% discount plus prices frozen at April 2004 rates for 4 years
- Some of the 70 affordable will be "super-affordable" (€100,000)
- Neighbourhood centre will be constructed
- Social regeneration funding (€3 m)
- Local labour clause

(Fatima Groups United, 2004a)

Finally, the selected consortium, Moritz/Elliot, started work on phase one of the social housing in the summer of 2004, and this was recently completed and officially launched on 3 October 2005.

In the case of St. Michael's Estate, after the agreed Master Plan was abandoned in 2003, a new Framework Plan was produced by Dublin City Council based on developing the site through a "public/private joint venture agreement" (Dublin City Council, 2004). This time, there was to be no community influence:

> Dublin City Council informed the St. Michael's Task Force they were engaging their own set of architects – that they would produce a Draft Framework Plan without us having any input...Dublin City Council did this alone from September 2003 to June 2004 (Fagan, 2004).

This plan aimed to reduce the public housing element of the estate from 346 to just 80 dwellings and increase the private to 770 (including 550 at full market price and 220 at an "affordable" or subsidized price). The new development was thus to include 850 units. It seems extraordinary that the council was again willing to dispose of a prime 14-acre site in return for so few public units at a time of considerable housing need and unaffordable land prices.

With very little on offer and without the same structures for engagement in place as existed in Fatima (i.e. the Regeneration Board), the community quickly organised a resistance movement, the "Save the St. Michael's/Inchicore Community Regeneration Plan". The central message of this campaign was the delivery of the original agreed plan (every campaign poster, petition, t-shirt, flyer and sticker carried the logo "don't let Dublin City Council stamp on our plan"). The campaign was launched with a public event, which was addressed by invited speakers and local people and culminated in the whole community delivering petitions and a copy of the existing agreed Master Plan to Civic Offices for the attention of the City Manager and Assistant City Manager. A petition was also carried out in the Inchicore area, collecting 3,200 signatures.

In September 2004, councillors in Dublin City Council voted unanimously on a motion to stop the plan for St. Michael's:

> [The] City Council rejects the proposed development for the lands of St. Michael's Estate, Inchicore and agrees, as part of the city's new plan, to consult again and create a new plan that is in accord with the clear views and aspirations of the local communities.

This was welcome given the extent of privatisation proposed and the very limited number of public units envisaged under the deal, as well as the fact that the process used to produce the plan abandoned the principle of local consultation. However, it also left the community in an extremely vulnerable situation at this point, faced with initial official statements that implied nothing would now happen on the estate[3].

Relations have since settled down and negotiations have been reinvigorated through the creation of a new Task Force. This local consultation continues at the time of writing – the formal PPP process (commencing with the RFP) is yet to begin. It will be some time before the final shape of the deal becomes clear, but it is to be hoped at the very least the outcomes for the remainder of the St. Michael's community, who have hung in there through years of stress and neglect, will be positive.

CONSIDERATIONS: SOCIAL PROGRESS OR SELLING THE CITY?

Such local experiences are in themselves important, but it is also necessary to take a step back and consider the broader implications of the evolution of urban regeneration and public housing policy in the city. It can be easy in a highly simplistic and uncritical way to present the demolition of public housing and the redevelopment of public land under a PPP as a great benefit for the city – particularly when the new projects are launched and the media and politicians turn up for a day – but such changes are not without considerable tensions and inequalities and serious questions can be asked about the real winners and losers. Indeed, despite some recent concerns about the appropriateness and value-for-money of public-private partnership (PPP) approaches to public service provision[4], there has been little debate or published research on the use of PPPs in the regeneration of public-housing areas (but see Kelly and MacLaran, 2004; Dillon, 2004). Yet such policies are already far-advanced in

Dublin, in what represents a radical departure in urban policy. The experience in these earliest projects – pioneer test sites for what is a new phase in public housing policy – deserves closer attention now and into the future.

As a useful starting point, some bottom-up insights will be made available through forthcoming community publications. These include an account of local experiences from Fatima Groups United (the first of these is due in late 2005) and a "Rough Guide to Regeneration" for communities from Tenants First (November 2005). In the context of an immediate and largely localised struggle[5], the communities discussed above have had to learn the language of planning, urban development and negotiation rapidly, and many have developed an important bottom-up understanding of the complexities of urban change and planning through these difficult and tense experiences. As well as the seminal community plans *Eleven Acres, Ten Steps* and *Past, Present, Future,* a remarkable series of presentations to two public conferences organised by, respectively, Dublin City Council and Threshold in November 2004 set out a challenging reading of urban development and city politics. In these sessions, the learning from Fatima, as well as O'Devaney Gardens (currently in the midst of PPP negotiations), was clearly articulated, while a presentation from St. Michael's Estate offered a more applied reading of the underlying processes and social relations at work and the nexus between power, knowledge and understanding. A further important critique was produced by Brian Dillon (2004), exploring how public-private partnership replaced community participation in the St. Michael's Estate case.

One could ask with a level of justifiable frustration: "but, is anybody listening?" Certainly, much needs to happen in order to move to a satisfactory, transparent and empowering approach to consultation and a progressive model of public housing and urban regeneration. Nevertheless, this considered approach is most necessary. In order to guard against Raymond Williams' (1989) problem of militant particularism[6], there is an urgent need to progress from local problems and actions to general ones, and this demands a broader analysis and consideration of policy, as well as careful monitoring of the PPP projects currently underway. What then are the general questions and understanding that can be drawn from Dublin City's recent engagement with market-driven housing strategies? The following social and economic questions deserve considered attention.

The Erosion of Social Housing

The public housing system in the city is under attack. This is happening on several fronts, notably the general under-development of public housing provision throughout the 1990s, the policy of selling off public land for private housing, the interpretation of Part V of the Planning & Development Act (in particular, the decision to require no additional social housing in 22 wards in the city), the recent suggestions coming from the local authority itself that it would seek to reduce its direct role as a public landlord and the PPP strategies outlined above, the most striking effect of which has been to reduce significantly the level of social housing in these local areas.

For example, if we consider again the case of Fatima, since funding collapsed for the earlier proposal, a dramatic shift in policies and priorities has quickly been revealed. In place of a scheme with considerable public investment, as well as some income-generating elements (mainly the private housing), the current plan is driven by the private sector, and the outcomes will largely depend on market forces. It seems inevitable that the private housing will be an intense development with densities of up to 120 units to the acre or more on some parts of the site, and it is predominantly to be located adjacent to a new light rail station, which opened at the end of June 2004. More striking still is the dilution of the public housing element and the escalation of the private. In the "old" Fatima, there were 394 housing units in public ownership (Dublin City Council, 2002); by the end of this whole process of negotiation, planning and PPP agreements, this will have been reduced by 62 per cent to a mere 150. In its place, the site is to take an intense increase of private dwellings. Table 6.2 makes the more recent erosion of social housing clear.

Table 6.2   Regeneration: the process of eroding social housing

Housing type	Fatima as constructed	Original Master Plan (2001)	Revised Master Plan (2002)	Preferred Bidder's Plan (2004)
Social	394	250	220	150
Private Market	0	Not specified	226	381
Private Affordable*	0	N/A	54	70
TOTAL	394	N/A	500	601

*Housing units to be sold at a subsidised (below-market) price for first-time buyers

Source: After Fatima Groups United (April, 2004b) *The value of a promise. The promise of value*, Dublin.

There is also a further dimension of this, which is not so readily apparent, regarding the long-term or inter-generational future of this locality. One concern is that the Fatima experiment is a predominantly market-driven scheme, which means it is impossible to predict what kind of new community will emerge in the private housing. Uncertainties abound regarding the stability or commitment to the area of the new community, the level of investor or speculator activity in the new apartments, the long-term social and cultural development of the area, and other such issues. In other words, there is great uncertainty as to the long-term social impact of these policies. The dependence on market forces to drive regeneration introduces considerable risk, as it leaves the whole outcome vulnerable to the vagaries of market cycles, thereby increasing uncertainty over such issues as private-sector commitment, design, phasing, location, social integration/ cohesion and long-term sustainability.

There are other uncertainties with regard to the public housing, however. The final deal agreed with the Fatima Regeneration Board included funding for a social-regeneration programme and very generous deals for local people in the shape of "super-affordable" housing and right-to-buy arrangements. It is worth noting that the latter two concessions will also encourage the further privatisation of the site. Throughout the engagement period, the ability of community representatives to fight the reduction in public housing or to influence the broader design of the new master plan was limited. One simple implication is that the remaining public-housing stock left in the area will be eroded further over coming years. Over a generation or two, it would seem likely that there will be relatively few local-authority tenants left in the "regenerated" Fatima (if that name itself survives at all). If this proves to be the case, the overall long-term meaning of regeneration will have as much to do with social clearance and gentrification as with improving the conditions of life for poorer and relatively powerless residents.

Broader policy concerns about the net loss of public housing should also be borne in mind. If housing policies, including regeneration policies, continue to erode the capacity of the city to respond directly to housing need, this raises worrying implications for low-income households now and into the future and concerns about inequality and housing access more broadly. This is particularly worrying given that Dublin City Council itself has stated that "the limited availability of land within the City boundaries for social housing presents a significant challenge" (Kenny, 2004). Yet the PPP model results in the privatisation of considerable amounts of scarce public land, as do the various policies for selling public land, houses and flats. To put the problem more starkly, what if the Fatima model was generalised to the entire public housing stock and remaining public land in the city? What would happen, in other words, if the city's public housing stock was reduced by 62 per cent?

Weak Economic Rationale

A clear evaluation of the financial rationale of this PPP model and comparisons with other options has not been carried out. Incredibly, in response to a question from the floor at a Dublin City Council conference in November 2004, it was admitted by the assistant city manager that the Council did not know the value of the land at St. Michael's Estate because they had not carried out any evaluation (Kelly and MacLaran, 2004).

The economic rationale behind some recent PPP agreements is even more unconvincing. The fact that the value of the St. Michael's site was allegedly not known was particularly astonishing given that a Framework Plan for a PPP redevelopment had already been drawn up (including just 80 social units) – though this was rejected following the grassroots campaign and the unanimous vote of the councillors. However, in response to a question put by Councillor Mick Rafferty to the City Manager (6.12.04), a valuation of €70 million was subsequently put on the main 11-acre site (not including the further 3 acres beside Emmett Road), that is, €6.3 million per acre. However, given its proximity to a Luas station and the current prices being fetched by inner city sites, this figure is very conservative. Allowing for the fact that the full 14-acre site would be likely to get permission for at least 1,000 units (an overall density of c. 70 per acre – lower than densities currently being achieved in the docklands and elsewhere), it would not be unreasonable to suggest that the site could fetch up to €140 million in the current market. The original proposed Framework Plan therefore would have been a good deal for the private partner given that the cost of providing 80 social units directly would have been at most €14 million (allowing a unit construction cost of €150,000) together with demolition and other costs.

What of Fatima Mansions? Again, it is a prime site – adjacent to a Luas station and Rialto. Arguably, the land value is at least €110 million given the site location and housing prices in the immediate area (new two-bed apartments in adjacent Cork Street were advertised at €380,000 in March 2004). This development will return 150 social units at a maximum cost to the developer of €22.5 million, while there will also be additional costs such as demolition, the provision of the community facility, landscaping, etc. Is this a good deal for the public?

The economic rationale also looks decidedly shaky from a broader conceptual perspective. The point is well made in the recent paper by Kelly and MacLaran (2004):

> As private-sector profitability has to be paid for, just how does the involvement of a private-sector partner *in addition to the building contractor* make for social efficiency in the operation of renewal? Where do the resources come from to provide the partner with the required profit? At a *given* level of input of resources, private-sector profitability may be derived from cost savings in three potential ways:
>
> a) By the private sector's ability to create *cost efficiencies in the management of renewal* when compared to in-house management by DCC staff. Such an argument for the use of PPPs would represent a clear statement of no confidence in DCC Housing Department's management abilities and is belied by the high quality of the renewal schemes already completed under its direction.

b) By the private sector's being able to gain access to *cheaper finance* than that available to public authorities. Given the public-sector's high credit rating, this is a highly unlikely scenario.

c) By *cost cutting* in terms of the quality of labour inputs and/or materials used. If this were possible, it might give considerable cause for concern over the quality of the final product created by the PPP arrangement.

In fact, it is more likely that the inclusion of any private-sector party in the regeneration process must create a need to expend *additional* resources to meet the private-sector's profitability requirements for engagement in the process. It is most likely that this requirement would be met by the *direct transfer of public-sector equity/value* to the PPP partner. This value transfer is most easily disguised and effected through the *transfer of land at a cost significantly below its market value*. Far from increasing the social efficiency of renewal schemes, PPPs are likely to embody an actual loss of value through the transfer of additional social resources to the private-sector partner (Kelly and MacLaran, 2004: 48).

The Limited Spectrum of Debate

The current vogue for PPPs in government (in evidence in various policy documents from 2000 onwards) has infected regeneration policies for public housing in a dramatic way since August 2003. This raises a broad policy concern: in place of a debate about what has gone wrong in decayed estates and an examination of all possible solutions, discussion is limited within a strategy of attracting private-sector interest. Instead, we need to evaluate and compare all possible approaches both to housing provision and regeneration: direct public investment in public housing, SWA for tenants of private landlords, remedial work schemes, voluntary-sector approaches, cross-subsidisation, cost rental, etc. There is no evidence that such an evaluation – either in terms of social benefit or value for money – has been carried out.

The local authority itself has admitted that there "are a number of options open to Dublin City Council for the site at St. Michael's (11 acres): -

1) Detenant the remaining residents (50) and sell the site on the open market without restriction
2) Retain part of the site (about 3-4 acres) to facilitate the construction of Social Housing and sell the remainder on the open market
3) Develop a comprehensive Masterplan for the site maximizing densities and including significant Social and Affordable housing and arrange the full construction directly by Dublin City Council
4) Continue the current P.P.P. process with strong influence by and restrictions placed by consultation and negotiation with the local community.

This latter option is the one being pursued (the effectiveness of the community influence remains to be seen); it is not clear why other, publicly-led approaches are not being evaluated or even considered.

Meaningful Public Participation and Community Input?

The nature and effectiveness of participation as pursued thus far is highly questionable. In any event, the experiences above have seriously damaged the credibility of such processes, given the extraordinary amount of wasted energy people expended in engaging in consultation about Master Plans for developments that would never be constructed.

This raises more complex questions about uneven power relations and about the location of decision-making authority and the openness of such authority to community input or influence. This issue is of even greater concern in a PPP context, where there is a realignment of control away from the state and towards market forces. This was well highlighted in

Brian Dillon's recent analysis of the St. Michael's case study (Dillon, 2004). In such an arrangement, the really key decisions are not always made in an open manner, nor are they easily open to any form of wider independent monitoring input, participation or democratic accountability.

The Real Lessons of History

Some council officials justify many of these market-driven policies on the grounds that earlier public housing policies have failed – the argument generally goes that any attempt to plot the way forward must learn from the experiences of the past, and this experience shows, it is alleged, that public housing does not work. There are two problems with this. First, it is not true, by and large. The history of public housing provision shows that social investment in both urban and rural areas has been enormously successful in ensuring people can access good housing, and many of the finest urban residential environments have been constructed in this way. It is sadly ironic that in the 1930s and 1950s, when this country was enduring a considerable depression, public investment in housing was at its peak, and the state was the majority housing provider. At the end of a period of unprecedented economic expansion, Dublin City Council is talking about (if not already actively proceeding with) the dismantlement of the system of public provision of housing instead of increasing its role. While there have been problems with public housing estates in the past, these derive from a combination of bad management and the everyday struggle with poverty (Fahey, 1999). Surely, it is naïve at best, and disingenuous at worst, to suggest that the underlying cause of such problems was housing tenure and that the reasoned response to these problems is to get rid of public housing altogether. Surely better management practices and anti-poverty strategies would provide more convincing solutions.

The second problem with arguing in favour of a return to 19th-century style market-driven housing policies and the reduction of public housing has to do with another lesson of history: the private sector has proven itself incapable of responding to all of the diverse housing needs of the population, above all the needs of low-income households and other marginalised groups. Experiences over 200 years with the private rental system should have taught us that a vibrant non-profit housing sector is an urgent requirement if our society is to ensure access to suitable housing and a reasonable quality of life for all. Sadly, the recent events in Dublin would suggest we are about to revive a policy direction that generated some of the worst housing slums in Europe in the 19th and early 20th century (Aalen 1992; Power, 1993).

Market-Driven Planning and Housing Policy: Who are the Winners and Losers?

In general, it is clear that these various changes in regeneration and housing policy have produced differential outcomes: sizable development profits can be extracted through the "creative destruction[7]" of the built environment by capital, with considerable encouragement from the state, while many indigeneous communities are less fortunate, being faced with the negative consequences (displacement, traffic congestion, segregated and exclusive development, etc.). Indeed, it could be argued that the state is now acting as a broker for capital in this process, while co-opting dissent and assuaging working-class combativity by diverting it into the safe channels of participatory and consultative structures. Once "on the inside" of such consultative committees or boards, it is likely that many tenants and community representatives will feel less able to speak critically about any of the policies or projects, however uneasy or alarmed they might be. Moreover, these consultation processes are not as a rule subject to much external scrutiny, nor do they greatly influence the outcome beyond a few marginal concessions (for example, the appropriateness or otherwise of a PPP demolition and redevelopment is never up for negotiation –

minor concessions within this framework might be won or lost, but the bigger project itself is beyond challenge).

CONCLUSION

In short, the housing and regeneration model applied is one wherein investment interests predominate over social concerns. In this situation, to regenerate local public-housing areas is code for the re-commodification of public land previously in use solely for housing for low-income families. Within this context, committed and well-organised grassroots action may win some concessions (such as the deal agreed in Fatima), but the long-term outcome and the broader implications for the city are at best equivocal. This raises practical concerns about housing access and inequality, but it also raises philosophical and political questions about the priorities of housing policy, the ideological commitments of policymakers and, perhaps most importantly of all, the meaning of urban regeneration and the underlying vision for the future of the city now being rapidly implemented. The discussion here is therefore just the slightest of starts. Certainly these experiences need to be revisited in more detail and the future sustainability and economic, social and cultural development of these localities need to be monitored very closely indeed.

Notes

1   About 300 households remained in Sheriff Street at this point out of an original 456. Much of the older community had been detenanted and relocated to peripheral housing estates over the previous decades of social decline. About 200 households were accommodated in the surrounding inner city areas by the local Authority.

2   Experiences in Fatima Mansions and St. Michael's Estate showed that this proactive approach is crucial if local people are to have any influence over future planning for the area

3   After the successful campaign and the unanimous vote, the assistant city manager, Brendan Kenny, was reported as saying "this is hugely disappointing and frustrating...As far as we're concerned it's dead and we have no plan at all now...We're not prepared to spend any more money on it" (*Irish Times,* 13 September 2004).

4   For example, the recent Comptroller and Auditor General Report on Value for Money Examination for the Department of Education and Science suggested that the Public Private Partnership experiment under the "Grouped Schools Project" (which was projected to achieve a saving of 6 per cent for the state) was in fact 13-19 per cent more expensive than traditional procurement approaches (Comptroller and Auditor General, 2004).

5   Though importantly, since November 2003, these and many other communities across the inner city have come together in a new urban social movement, Tenants First, with the aim of providing a strong collective voice for local tenants on issues relating to their living and housing conditions. It aims to provide support, advice and a space for tenant representatives to come together and share mutual experiences and concerns and to develop responses and actions.

6   Williams argued that the key difficulty for a progressive politics lay in bringing local struggles for social justice together into a general platform or movement. Too often, such local actions – "militant particularisms" – remained at a local level and often foundered, became inward looking and defensive, or even became quite regressive in aims and focus (as "NIMBY" approaches often are, for instance).

7   An apt phrase for the long process of "regeneration" continuing across the inner city. Constellations of capital and state agencies first down-graded inner-city areas over decades through restructuring, disinvestment and decentralisation policies and then returned to recommodify the devalued spaces. In short, in a dialectical sense the decay and the renewal are the two broad moments in the long process of urban change and cannot be disentangled.

Chapter 7

Models of Best
Practice in Housing

In this book our contention is that housing provision and policy in Ireland have been heavily influenced by a market-driven philosophy. The vast brunt of current provision is for sale for profit or for speculative purposes and in recent years the state has increasingly encouraged this trend. Housing is, in the main, perceived as and treated as a commodity, like televisions, motor cars or stocks and shares to be traded on the market and a means of wealth creation. Those with resources or access to credit are able to purchase or rent homes, although increasing numbers do so with considerable difficulty since there is virtually no control over escalating prices and rents. Furthermore, in the Irish market sector there is little control over the quality of housing and there is no apparent consumer protection. This is the market in action and, as illustrated earlier, it has done very little for those who have few resources. It creates serious difficulties even for those who are relatively well-off. The level of indebtedness arising from this situation remains a matter of serious national concern (Central Bank and Financial Services Authority of Ireland, 2005).

In Ireland land is a scarce but critical resource in relation to housing, especially in the main urban centres. Its allocation and price is also left to an imperfect monopolistic market where relatively few landowners, developers and speculators can accumulate land over a period of years and thus exert considerable control over supply. The re-zoning of land and the giving of planning permission for housing by Local Authorities are the final mechanisms which make large unearned financial gains for one privileged group. In the process, the state becomes responsible for the provision of services.

The European Union has of course over many years applauded the merits of the market system. Indeed, the original Treaty of Rome in 1957 clearly underlined and emphasised the precedence of that philosophy. Even from the beginning, however, this pure philosophy was diluted by a range of policy "derogations" arising from fundamental social concerns such as low incomes, high unemployment, poverty and regional disparities and the well-known reality of regular "market failure". The recent rejection of the proposed European Constitution by France and the Netherlands and the abandonment (at least in the short term) of that aspiration by other member states is a reflection of the widespread public concern about the headlong rush towards further integration and with it the further strengthening of a market orientation. This circumspection is to be welcomed. We would put it as follows : The market has a place, but it must be kept in its place! When we examine housing and land in a range of European countries and further afield, we find that market forces can indeed play an important role. We also find, however, that in most countries the market is not generally allowed to dominate to the extent that it has done in Ireland. Home ownership is certainly encouraged but house price and rent inflation is not, and those who have not the resources to enter the home ownership or private rental markets are catered for with a variety of innovative measures throughout Europe, Scandinavia and further afield. In this chapter, we discuss several key concepts and initiatives which are widely believed to be essential for "good" housing systems and which, in our view, offer useful lessons for policy and practice in Ireland. First, however, we argue that these concepts and initiatives should be based on a legally established right to housing.

SITUATING HOUSING POLICY IN A RIGHTS FRAMEWORK

The moral justification for a right to housing is grounded in the fundamental importance of housing and shelter to a decent human existence and to human flourishing. The right to housing is not only an intrinsic component of the right to life but is essential to the enjoyment of other rights which themselves are universally recognised as fundamental. These include the right to health, to marry and found a family, to privacy, to education, to participate in economic, social and public life.

The right to housing is long-established in a wide range of international human rights instruments. First stated in the United Nations' *Universal Declaration of Human Rights* in 1948, the right to housing has been explicitly restated and amplified in a series of subsequent international human rights conventions, including the *International Covenant on Economic, Social and Cultural Rights* (adopted by the United Nations General Assembly in 1966), the *Convention on the Elimination of All Forms of Discrimination Against Women* (1979); the *Convention on the Rights of the Child* (1989) and the *International Convention on the Protection of the Rights of Migrant Workers and Members of their Families* (1990). These conventions articulate internationally accepted standards and illustrate the sustained global support given to the right to adequate housing by the international community (Kenna, 2002, 2005). Ireland is a party both to the *Universal Declaration* and to all these conventions.

Article 25 of the *Universal Declaration* states that:

> Everyone has the right to a standard of living adequate for the health and well-being of himself (herself) and his (her) family, including food, clothing, housing, medical care and necessary social services...

Article 11 of the *International Covenant on Economic, Cultural and Social Rights* is as follows:

> The States Parties to the present Covenant recognise the right of everyone to an *adequate* standard of living for himself/herself and his/her family, including adequate food, clothing and housing and to the continuous improvement of living conditions. The States Parties will take appropriate steps to ensure the realisation of this right ... (emphasis added)

The UN Committee on Economic, Social and Cultural Rights, the body responsible for monitoring States Parties' compliance with the obligations they have assumed under the Covenant on Economic, Social and Cultural Rights, has spelled out in some detail what is meant by the term "adequate housing". This must be affordable, habitable and accessible to disadvantaged groups. It should include security of tenure, availability of services, materials, facilities and infrastructure. Its location must allow access to employment, health care, schools, child care centres and other social facilities (United Nations Office of the High Commissioner for Human Rights, 1991).

By becoming a party to the *International Covenant on Economic, Social and Cultural Rights*, and the other more recent treaties referred to above, Ireland has consciously recognised at an international level the rights they contain, including specifically the right to housing. Moreover, it has accepted the related obligation to report at regular intervals to the appropriate UN monitoring bodies on how it is discharging its obligations under the treaty in question. For example, it was examined by the UN Committee on

Economic, Social and Cultural Rights on its performance in implementing the *International Covenant on Economic, Social and Cultural Rights* in May 1999 and again in 2002

In its *Concluding Observations* on Ireland's *Second Periodic Report* in 2002, the Committee expressed its concern that:

- many new households in Ireland could not secure adequate and affordable housing,
- some 1,200 families of the Travelling Community were living in roadside encampments without access to water and adequate sanitary facilities and were liable to be forcefully evicted, and
- a large number of people with mental disabilities whose state of health would allow them to live in the community were still accommodated in psychiatric hospitals. (E/C 12/1/Add. 77, 2002)

An overarching concern of the Committee was that despite the recommendation it had made following its examination of Ireland's *First Periodic Report* in 1999, "no steps have been taken (by Ireland) to incorporate or reflect the Covenant in domestic legislation". This reflects the emphasis which the Committee places on the fact that States Parties are under an obligation to develop an appropriate legal framework to give full effect to the rights in the Covenant at national level.

One of the main objections to a juridically enforceable right to housing is that it would leave the state open to unrealistic demands on resources. However, neither the UN nor the majority of those who endorse a right to housing understand it as an unlimited or unqualified claim on the state's resources. There are few, if any, rights, whether civil and political or economic and social, which are not in practice subject in one way or another to resource constraints. The interpretation and implementation of a juridically recognised right to housing would therefore be qualified in certain respects by the availability of resources. What a legal recognition of a right to housing would achieve, however, would be greater protection for vulnerable groups within the overall resource limitations to which the state is always subject.

Aside from this, adequate juridical recognition of a right to housing would allow better enjoyment of the right in ways which require little or no resources. These would include strengthened procedural rights related to housing, such as the right not to be discriminated against, rights to appeal, to redress and due process in general, and rights to information and consultation.

It should also be emphasised that juridical recognition of a right to housing need not result in replacing the role of the market. This would remain as one means by which many people would expect to secure their right to housing. However, grounding overall housing policy in a rights framework would ensure a better balance between market and non-market approaches to meeting housing needs. It would shift the centre of gravity of policy, so that the most vulnerable would have more effective legal protection and meeting their needs would command a higher priority in public policy-making and provision (Whyte, 2002).

It is worth pointing out also that failure to ensure that everyone enjoys a right to housing imposes substantial costs on the state and the community as a whole, apart from its impact on those directly affected. Homelessness and inadequate housing result in significant economic and social costs in terms of family instability, additional demands on health services, lost productivity as a result of an inability to participate fully in education and employment, and the exclusion of people from active participation in the community.

Many countries have now incorporated the right to housing into their Constitutions or in legislation. Housing is already a constitutional right in South Africa, Sweden, Finland, Belgium, Greece, the Netherlands, Portugal and

Spain. Three of these countries (Finland, Sweden and Portugal) have also established the right by legislation. There is also a legal right in Austria, France, Germany, Denmark and Luxembourg (BIPE, 2000; CECODHAS, 2005).

A significant number of Irish agencies and trade unions, including the Combat Poverty Agency, Threshold, the Simon Community, the Irish Commission for Justice and Peace, the Civil and Public Services Union and SIPTU, have all stressed the need for housing to be treated as a fundamental human right (CPSU and SIPTU, 1998; Connolly, 1998; Combat Poverty Agency, 1999; Threshold, 2002; CORI, 2004, 2005). It must, of course, be emphasised that incorporating a right to housing in the Constitution would not in itself guarantee adequate implementation of such a right. As with practically all constitutionally recognised rights, it would require in practice to be spelled out in statute law and implemented through a range of appropriate policies, administrative structures and financial programmes. Granting a juridical right to housing would, nevertheless, signal a clear commitment to providing housing appropriate to the needs of everyone, particularly those without the necessary resources to buy or rent on the private market (Connolly, 2002, 2004; Punch and Drudy, 2002; Burns, 2005).

At the present time the dominant philosophy of the Government in Ireland appears to be strongly opposed to rights-based legislation. However, it is encouraging to note that in its 2004 Report on Private Property, the All Party Oireachtas Committee on the Constitution, in response to the numerous submissions it had received which argued for a right to shelter and/or housing, accepted that this issue merited consideration by the Committee and it stated its intention to examine socio-economic rights, including the right to housing, in a later report (All-Party Oireachtas Committee on the Constitution, 2004, p. 19).

In any case, we argue that there is an increasingly unacceptable contradiction between the Irish State's overt acceptance of a right to housing through its ratification of major international human rights treaties, on the one hand, and, on the other, its continuing refusal to reflect these obligations in appropriate constitutional and legislative provision at domestic level. It would be unthinkable that the Irish State would resolve this contradiction by withdrawing from the international treaties in question. The contradiction can only be resolved, by giving domestic recognition to the rights which the country continues to proclaim at international level.

TOWARDS AN INTEGRATED AND BALANCED TENURE PATTERN

As will be clear from this book, the various housing tenures in Ireland have tended to be treated separately. Home ownership has been given particular attention, the private rental sector has been largely neglected until recently and public housing has been relegated to a residual position. In effect, the system is a 'segregated' one. This division is not so stark in other western European countries where rental housing is much more prevalent and where there is a less dominant market orientation. Kemeny has drawn a useful distinction between what he calls a 'unitary' (unified) system and a 'dualist' (segregated) system with contrasting policies (Kemeny, 1995). While Kemeny was referring mainly to private and public rental housing, the distinction can be applied more broadly to a housing system as a whole.

In dualist models, a profit-driven market is supported and protected from competition from non-profit providers. There is likely to be a strong emphasis on promoting private ownership as an essential goal of policy. In some cases, the private rental system (as opposed to the public one) is also given an important role. Public provision is downgraded or residualised to a welfare role, providing a safety net for some, but not all, of the casualties of the profit market.

In this approach, public housing is thus separated from the housing market in general, protected and regulated to keep rents low, and targeted through means-testing to the most needy groups (Davidson, 1999, p.456). This has the added negative consequence of a considerable degree of stigmatisation and segregation of the sector.

By contrast, in a unitary system, an integrated and tenure-neutral approach ensures a range of housing options, both public and private. Public rental housing is allowed to prosper, involving widespread non-profit provision for "general needs" and not just for the most needy groups. It thus can compete with private development and play a price-leading role. This model can therefore help to dampen down price escalation and stabilise the housing system and the economy in general. Cost-rental models (where rents cover the cost of borrowing) are promoted, and over the long term, these can operate more efficiently and equitably by exploiting the benefits of rent pooling across a mature stock. Eventually (when the borrowing is repaid), this enables investment in further housing. This policy of building up a mature stock (termed "maturation" by Kemeny) is critical to success and contrasts with policies of selling off public housing. It can be argued that this long-term approach also improves rental accessibility, increases flexibility, de-stigmatises public housing and improves housing choice regardless of income.

In a unitary system the availability and price of land may be strategically controlled in the interests of the community through measures such as public land banking, a policy which should reduce or eliminate speculative activity. The Vienna Land Procurement and Urban Renewal Fund in Vienna and the tradition of public land banking in Sweden offer good examples (Barlow and Duncan, 1994; Forster, 1996; Turner, 1996). Kemeny identifies Britain, Australia and New Zealand (one could also add Ireland) as typical examples of largely "dualist" housing systems, whereas Sweden, the Netherlands, Germany and Switzerland have adopted "unitary" approaches to varying extents.

Most European countries have a rather more balanced and regulated tenure pattern than in Ireland. Thus, most have relatively high proportions either in the private or public rental sectors and many have a stronger regulatory system than in Ireland. Compared to a low proportion of less than 7 per cent public housing in Ireland, Sweden, Denmark and the Netherlands have 24 per cent, 27 per cent and 35 per cent respectively. Public housing therefore represents an obvious option for a significant section of the population. In relation to private renting, the proportions here range from 11 per cent in the Netherlands to 51 per cent in Germany. Yet there is a tradition and widespread acceptance of the need for rent regulation in a range of countries and the indexing of rent increases. Most EU countries have moved towards a system that allows some type of rent indexation to consumer price inflation and the typical rental contract reflects this. In Denmark, Sweden and France, for example, indexation is linked to housing costs. Germany likewise has an adjustment mechanism that allows increases in rents of sitting tenants up to a maximum of 20 per cent over three years (European Central Bank, 2003). This "second generation" rent regulation works in the interests of both landlord and tenant. Thus, there are clear and often very attractive alternatives to home ownership for the tenant, and landlords can be assured of viable long-term tenancies. The quest for home ownership, if it ever arises, can be postponed for a considerable period, thus reducing the pressure of demand and the extent of resulting house price increases.

SUSTAINABLE DEVELOPMENT, HOUSING AND COMMUNITIES

There is widespread acceptance that a housing system should be "sustainable", although this term can interpreted in a variety of ways. There is similarly broad agreement on the need for "sustainable communities". In Ireland, the term sustainable housing has tended to be used in a relatively narrow sense to include "high density" residential development along public transport routes – this interpretation places the emphasis on "urban design". High density housing (which is not necessarily high rise) in appropriate locations can indeed contribute to sustainability, but cannot on its own make up a "good quality of life" for the inhabitants (a key element in "sustainable development"). Real sustainability would involve much more, possibly including physical change but also appropriate economic, social, environmental and cultural elements. While perfect examples of sustainable communities are difficult to identify, we can draw on a range of key international studies (e.g. European Commission, 1999; European Ministers, 2002; Power, 2004; Bannon, 1981 and 2005) to identify a number of commonly-used criteria to define whether housing communities are sustainable or not. These include:

- *Affordability*: the cost of housing should not compromise other essential needs such as nutrition, health, education, cultural development
- *Accessibility*: for those with low incomes or homeless and those with physical or intellectual disabilities
- *Viable economy*: appropriate employment in a range of activities located locally or within reasonable distance by public transport
- *Minimal commuting by car*: Long distance car commuting is inimical to community development and cohesion. It is wasteful of energy and time
- *Healthy and safe environment*: Minimal waste and pollution, protection and enhancement of the natural environment, safe and secure environment
- *Appropriate environment*: contains good range of social, recreational, educational, child-care, cultural facilities, good quality open spaces/green areas

- *Eco-efficient and adaptable*: minimal energy consumption, innovative construction methods, lifelong adaptable construction
- *Quality of life*: social well-being and inclusion, sense of security, belonging, support, cohesion, integration of different social groups based on respect for different cultures and traditions

It may be noted that there is a marked similarity between these criteria and those identified by the UN Committee on Economic, Social and Cultural Rights as core elements in the right to adequate housing outlined earlier.

BALANCED URBAN AND REGIONAL FRAMEWORK

Practically every country in the world now aspires to have "balanced urban and regional development". While the emphasis differs from country to country, the common thread is that there is both an economic and social case for policies which attempt to spread population and economic activity in a reasonable manner throughout the national territory. If this does not occur, there will be an inevitable tendency for certain areas to grow and others to decline. The growth areas (invariably towns and cities) will accrue a range of benefits but in due course will experience "diseconomies of agglomeration" in the form of high land and house prices, long-distance commuting, pressures on amenity land, pollution and traffic congestion. On the other hand, the areas distant from the centres of growth fail to realise their potential for sustainable development in their own right. Instead, many of them become dormitory towns for daily long-distance commuters, without the necessary infrastructure, employment and facilities necessary for sustainability. This is not sustainable development.

In most European countries, the difficulties outlined

above are taken seriously and genuine attempts are made to spread population and activity away from the dominant centres (European Commission, 1999). Despite lip service in Ireland over many years to the concept of 'balanced urban and regional development', the gap between the "Eastern Core" and the "Western Periphery" has increased consistently (see, for example, Bannon, 2004a, 2004b, 2004c; Drudy and MacLaran, 2004). In 1969 the Buchanan Report (1969) recommended the development of nine 'growth centres'" as well as a number of secondary centres around the country to act as 'counter magnets' to the growing Dublin area. Due to political considerations, the proposal was shelved. While some of the proposed growth centres grew, a positive policy approach was never put in place, although numerous studies have argued for such an approach since then. In 2002, after several years of study, a *National Spatial Strategy* was published (Government of Ireland, 2002). Similar to the Buchanan report, it proposed the development of eight major centres (termed "gateways") and eleven smaller centres (termed "hubs") throughout the country, although it surprisingly argued that Dublin should at the same time be allowed to grow. Shortly afterwards, the then Minister for Finance, Mr Charlie McCreevy, proposed a major programme of decentralisation for the civil service involving 53 towns, many of these having no linkages at all with the *National Spatial Strategy*. In 2005, as we go to print, a major debate is underway concerning these two conflicting approaches – one which logically 'concentrates' development in a limited number of towns and the other which unwisely 'disperses' activity widely throughout the nation and which has little or no support from those employed in the civil service.

LAND: A CRITICAL RESOURCE

A factor of central importance to a good housing system is

the availability and price of land suitable for housing, together with the servicing of such land with water, sewage, drainage and waste management. Indeed, the availability of land at a reasonable cost is essential if a right to housing is to become a reality. There is little doubt that in Ireland the price of land can represent a significant proportion of housing costs and is thus is a key determinant of the rise in house prices. Even when land is purchased at "existing use" prices (e.g. as agricultural land) it is the "development land price" (after re-zoning and planning permission) that is generally built into the price of the house. In any case, the exceptional increases in the price of land (whether real or apparent) are invariably passed on to house purchasers in the form of higher house prices.

The availability of land at a reasonable price for housing, especially in the main urban centres, has been a deep cause of concern in Ireland for almost three decades. In the early 1970s, this concern resulted in the establishment of a Committee on the Price of Building Land under the chairmanship of Mr. Justice Kenny. The main objective was to find a way to stabilise or reduce the price of building land and to ensure that the community acquired on fair terms the 'betterment' element which arises from works carried out by Local Authorities. The Committee reported to the Government in 1973 (Kenny, 1973). The main proposal was that Local Authorities should be enabled to acquire potential housing land designated by the High Court at 'existing use value' plus 25 per cent. This proposal inevitably raised objections, and in particular it was argued that it was an 'unjust attack' on property rights and was therefore contrary to the Constitution. The Constitution of Ireland (1937) states that:

> The State shall, in particular, by its laws protect as best it may from unjust attack and, in the case of injustice done, vindicate the life, person, good name and property rights of every citizen (Article 40.3.2)

This view was far from universal, however, on the grounds that the rights of property owners must be regulated by 'principles of social justice' and the 'common good' – also set out in the Constitution (see Articles 43.2.1 and 43.2.2). The All Party Oireachtas Committee on the Constitution (2004) likewise concluded that the acquisition of land at its existing use value in the interests of the common good was in conformity with the Constitution – a conclusion also reached by the Supreme Court in relation to Part V of the 2000 Planning Act several years previously. See *Article 26 and the Planning and Development Bill, 1999*, Re [2000] IESC 20. The enactment of legislation which clearly and adequately reflects Articles 43.2.1 and 43.2.2 (dealing with the principles of social justice and the common good respectively) would resolve this problem. The legislation should specify that land required for housing, either for rent or for sale, can be purchased by the state at existing use value plus a reasonable addition for disturbance.

The Austrian and Swedish experiences are instructive and relevant. In Austria, the Vienna Land Procurement and Urban Renewal Fund, an Arbitration Committee and Area Renewal Offices play strong roles in moderating market forces and in relation to acquiring land in the city in order to control land prices and to facilitate the development of affordable housing. Speculative activity is largely removed because these public bodies co-ordinate all stages of housing development, whether private or public, from zoning to disposal of sites to housing promotion and infrastructural delivery. These public bodies thus play a very important role in people-centred urban renewal (Economic Commission for Europe, 1998).

In Sweden there is a major emphasis on public land banking. This helps to control land allocation, land prices and house prices. Price is regulated by special land tribunals, and most building is financed by state housing loans, but to get such a loan, a limit is put on the price to be paid for land

and housing. In Sweden, the non-profit sector is responsible for 50 per cent of completions. A large share is also provided by restricted-profit provision, with speculative development only accounting for a small percentage of housing output (NESC, 2004: Background Report, no. 7). A comparison between Sweden, France and Britain showed that Sweden had the highest level of productive efficiency and responsiveness so that land was readily available at relatively low prices, generating certainty for builders. Price regulation ensures that consumers benefit in terms of housing costs and quality. The major source of profit for developers lies in production efficiency and innovation rather than from inflated land or house prices. Similarly in the Netherlands, local authorities are key buyers in the land market. They prepare land for building and then sell or lease. They make land available to housing associations at low prices for social housing (Needham and De Kam, 2000).

Chapter 8

Conclusions: Re-instating Housing as a Home

In this book, we have argued that housing analysis and policy in Ireland over recent years have been under-pinned by a dominant paradigm, which has placed enormous emphasis on market provision and downgraded the role of the state. In effect, this has led to the commodification of what should be treated as an important social good, like health or education. This unbalanced policy emphasis has created significant difficulties for many people, particularly with regard to housing access, while the almost exclusive reliance on "the market" as a provider has influenced many others to see housing as means of speculation and wealth creation rather than a shelter and a home.

How then can we make progress? We set out below a number of key principles which should, in our view, guide future housing policy and we make a small number of recommendations for policy change.

KEY PRINCIPLES AND POLICIES FOR A PROGRESSIVE HOUSING SYSTEM:

• Principles
★ Housing should be treated as a social good, rather than

as a commodity for trading or wealth generation. Housing policies should clearly reflect this principle.

★ Housing is a fundamental economic and social need; everyone should have a right to affordable housing appropriate to needs. The right to housing should be established in legislation in line with signed international covenants and agreements.

★ Since land is a fundamental requirement in relation to housing provision and co-ordinated planning, the state should have a long-term strategy of land acquisition at existing use value plus a percentage for disturbance in order to meet at a reasonable price the needs of both market and non-market providers and to ensure that the necessary social infrastructure and amenities are made available without delay.

• National Housing Authority

In order to give housing the priority and status it deserves, there is a strong case for establishing a new National Housing Authority to oversee, co-ordinate and facilitate high quality housing provision, as recommended by the National Economic and Social Forum some years ago. The new Authority could build on existing expertise in the Department of Environment, Heritage and Local Government, the Local Authorities and in the Housing Associations and Co-operatives. As well as working closely with Local Planning Authorities, the Housing Authority should have strong input at a local community level to advise on housing needs and broader related concerns in particular areas. One of its first tasks should be the provision of a comprehensive Urban, Regional and Rural Housing Strategy.

• Urban, Regional and Rural Housing Strategy

In order to avoid ad hoc provision of housing throughout the country without appropriate planning and relevant infrastructure, a Housing Strategy should be put in place in relation to housing needs and provision in different parts of the country. This Strategy must be in line with the Government's *National Spatial Strategy* designed to take pressure off the 'eastern core' of the country.

- Sustainable Housing and Communities

A good housing system will not be achieved by the provision of physical units of housing alone. The emphasis must shift to sustainable development and to improving the quality of life for the occupants of homes. This requires a comprehensive holistic approach. In line with sustainability principles, provision today should not compromise potential for future generations. Housing should be affordable, accessible and should involve minimal commuting to employment. It should be in a safe and appropriate environment with adequate social, recreational and other facilities for adults and children. It should facilitate and contribute to social well-being, inclusion and community development.

- House Price and Rent Inflation

A sustained level of private housing supply is needed to dampen down market prices and rents in line with normal inflationary trends, but it is also essential to ensure a significant increase in all non-market housing, including a proposed community housing tenure, in order to create competition (see below). It is clear from this book that much of the current market supply is being taken up by investors and speculators. To deal with this problem, there is a case for the elimination of mortgage interest relief and a significant increase in capital gains tax for those purchasing second or further homes for speculative purposes. Furthermore, there is a strong case for the termination of a range of tax incentives such as Section 23/27 which contribute to speculative demand and to house prices. Lending institutions should be subject to more rigorous regulations in relation to sustainable borrowing levels. Prices and rents are unlikely to stabilise unless there is a good supply of zoned and serviced land available at a reasonable price. Therefore, a major programme of state acquisition of land for both market and non-market housing is essential. Orderly acquisition and allocation by the state would ensure certainty for all providers and would offer greater prospects of co-ordinated planning and implementation.

• New Community Housing Tenure

The current Local Authority stock provides homes for a narrow group of the population on low incomes, many of them suffering from unemployment, educational disadvantage and other difficulties and thus paying relatively low rents. Apart from the undesirable segregation and concentration of a particular social group in certain areas, this contributes to financial instability of the remaining stock. There is a case, therefore, for establishing a new broadly-based housing tenure called "community housing" which would cater for a much wider range of housing need as well as existing Local Authority tenants. It would thus include relatively well-off tenants who do not currently wish to purchase homes or are not yet in a position to do so, but who are able to pay an economic rent, at least sufficient to cover maintenance and other costs associated with the home – along the lines of a 'cost rental' model – thus enabling this new tenure to become and remain financially viable. This tenure would have the potential to be a competitor with the private market, thus dampening down price inflation. In addition, this new tenure could make a considerable contribution to the aim of achieving integration and to reducing social segregation. In the light of the estimated housing need given earlier in this book, there is a requirement for at least 10,000 financially viable non-profit housing units per annum over the next decade, including the proposed community housing, and those provided by housing associations and co-operatives. This target was proposed by us in

1999 (Drudy et al 1999) and was again recommended by the National Economic and Social Council in December 2004 (NESC, 2004).

- **Terminate the Sale of Local Authority Housing**

The sale of public housing over many years has reduced the stock in a significant manner. The scheme represents a substantial subsidy to the better-off tenants and contributes to the marginalisation and residualisation of the remaining reduced stock. A residual stock with a high proportion of low income tenants means a consequent reduction in rental income and the weakening of long-term viability through "maturation". Further sales would also result in a fall in the number of annual vacancies which heretofore made a significant contribution towards the growing waiting list. The sale of public housing should therefore be discontinued, but tenants wishing to purchase homes should receive particular assistance and encouragement to use the existing shared ownership and affordable housing schemes.

- **Reform in the Private Rented Sector**

The passing of the Private Residential Tenancies Act in 2004 and the establishment of the Private Residential Tenancies Board are likely to be beneficial to both tenants and landlords. However, there is still room for reform. This sector offers a housing option for relatively well-off tenants seeking to meet short-term accommodation needs. Nevertheless, there is a strong case for the introduction of more rent certainty for these and other tenants through a system of rent indexation related to inflation trends and to account for improvements. However, this is not a satisfactory option for tenants on low incomes, including those eligible for rent supplement. Much rental accommodation for such tenants has been expensive and continues to be of low standard and the local authorities have so far failed to ensure that basic standards required by law are maintained.

The proposal to provide long-term accommodation in the private rental sector for those on long-term rent supplement via a Residential Accommodation Scheme (RAS) should therefore be re-considered. The significant annual expenditure on rent supplement (in excess of €350 million per annum) should be diverted instead into the proposed community housing tenure.

Tax incentives such as Section 23/27 have existed and have been renewed repeatedly over several decades. They are deeply regressive and represent a large and unjustified subsidy to investors, speculators and owner-occupiers. A case could be made for their retention in cases where new rental accommodation is required and provided at regulated rents for low income groups. They should be terminated for all other groups.

• Special Needs
In this book we have briefly examined three groups with special needs - homeless people, travellers and people with disabilities. The elderly are also an important and deserving group with special requirements. These are among the most vulnerable in Irish society and special housing arrangements and provision is essential for them. In particular, access to permanent and appropriate accommodation must become the central focus of policy. There are many examples of 'best practice' from individuals homes to group housing schemes in community settings with the necessary back-up services and facilities to ensure ongoing security and general well-being. Future housing assessments and strategies should give a high priority to such groups.

• Land Acquisition Programme
The limited availability and high price of land has contributed to the relentless rise in both house prices and rents, while also limiting the ability of non-profit providers to produce sufficient levels of social-housing units. High land

prices would also inhibit the success of the proposed community housing model described above. Given that land is one of the critical resources required for housing, whether for sale or rent, the state has a duty to acquire sufficient land at a reasonable cost, and therefore should develop a significant programme of state acquisition without further delay. Such land could then be released in a planned and orderly fashion to private and social housing providers as required.

- Substantial Land Tax on Windfall Profit

In view of the housing shortages and unmet housing need, a strong case can be made that landowners should not accrue significant unearned gains purely as a result of land re-zoning or changes in planning permission. Such planning permission always brings a responsibility to provide services; yet land owners often make little or no contribution to these. One possible corrective is a substantial land tax or a capital gains tax on "unearned" price increases on land that has been zoned and serviced for development. At present, actions taken by the state on behalf of the community (e.g. via re-zoning, planning permission or the provision of infrastructure) too often simply result in enormous profits to landowners who bear none of the costs of residential development. The potential for such windfall gains in return for no productive activity whatsoever is totally unwarranted and leaves the planning system open to corruption (Flood, 2002a, 2002b).

In conclusion we need to bluntly ask ourselves whether the first priority of the Irish housing system should be the realisation of investment, speculative, or capital gains by those with the necessary resources, or the provision of an affordable, secure, good-quality home as the basic right of every citizen? Simply put, are houses in the final analysis a market commodity, or comfortable shelter from the storm? The choice, either way, is ours.

Appendix Tables

Table A1   Average House (including apartments) prices

YEAR	NEW HOUSES		SECOND- HAND HOUSES	
	Dublin area	Whole country	Dublin area	Whole country
	€	€	€	€
1974	10,943	10,836	11,777	11,817
1975	13,137	13,254	12,774	12,478
1976	15,342	15,564	15,850	15,303
1977	19,055	18,754	18,778	17,925
1978	25,745	24,082	22,920	21,895
1979	32,005	29,387	30,092	27,598
1980	37,822	34,967	34,129	30,927
1981	44,456	40,167	42,193	37,394
1982	48,886	44,060	45,912	40,308
1983	48,169	44,448	48,249	43,204
1984	48,819	45,419	50,936	45,208
1985	49,166	46,542	50,382	45,608
1986	50,891	48,256	51,450	47,082
1987	50,864	48,151	49,139	46,330
1988	57,994	52,450	54,077	50,501
1989	68,393	58,178	63,148	54,586
1990	80,749	65,541	74,833	62,387
1991	78,715	66,914	76,075	64,122
1992	79,200	69,264	77,490	65,331
1993	75,539	69,883	76,814	66,736
1994	81,993	72,732	82,772	69,877
1995	86,671	77,994	88,939	74,313
1996	97,058	87,202	104,431	85,629
1997	122,036	102,222	131,258	102,712
1998	160,699	125,302	176,420	134,529

1999	193,526	148,521	210,610	163,316
2000	221,724	169,191	247,039	190,550
2001	243,095	182,863	267,939	206,117
2002	256,109	198,087	297,424	227,799
2003	291,646	224,567	355,451	264,898
2004	322,628	249,191	389,791	294,667

Source: Department of the Environment, 2005

Notes:-
(a) Prior to 1974 the data was based on surveys of existing house sales in Dublin carried out by the Valuation Office on behalf of the D. O. E. Since 1974 the data has been based on information supplied by all lending agencies on the average price of mortgage financed existing house transactions.
(b) Average house prices are derived from data supplied by the mortgage lending agencies on loans approved by them. In comparing house prices figures from one period to another, account should be taken of the fact that changes in the mix of houses (including apartments) will affect the average figures.

Table A2   Owner Occupied Housing Units by Regional Authority, 2002

	With Mortgage	Without Mortgage	Total
Dublin	153,316	101,991	255,307
Mid East	61,690	39,860	101,550
Midlands	26,429	29,380	55,809
Mid West	39,902	44,351	84,253
Border	48,833	60,297	109,130
South East	47,891	55,537	103,428
South West	66,113	75,345	141,458
West	40,600	54,405	95,005
Total	484,774	461,166	945,940

Source: *Census of Population*, 2002

Table A3 Population by Region (000s) and Regional Shares in Ireland (%), 1961-2002

Region	1961	1971	1981	1986	1991	1996	2002
DUBLIN							
Population	719.0	852.2	1003.2	1021.4	1025.3	1058.3	1122.8
Regional Share (%)	25.5	28.6	29.1	28.9	29.1	29.2	28.7
MID-EAST							
Population	187.0	200.0	287.0	313.7	325.2	347.4	412.6
Regional Share	6.6	6.7	8.3	8.9	9.2	9.6	10.5
SOUTHWEST							
Population	446.9	465.7	525.2	536.6	532.3	546.6	580.4
Regional Share	15.9	15.6	15.3	15.2	15.1	15.1	14.8
SOUTHEAST							
Population	319.9	328.6	374.6	384.7	383.2	391.5	423.6
Regional Share	11.4	11	10.9	10.9	10.9	10.8	10.8
MID-WEST							
Population	260.7	269.8	308.2	315.0	310.7	317.1	339.6
Regional Share	9.3	9.1	8.9	8.9	8.8	8.7	8.7
MIDLANDS							
Population	180.1	178.9	202.2	207.8	203.0	205.5	225.4
Regional Share	6.4	6.0	5.8	5.9	5.8	5.7	5.8
WEST							
Population	332.4	312.2	341.3	347.8	343.0	352.4	380.3
Regional Share	11.8	10.5	9.9	9.8	9.7	9.7	9.7
BORDER							
Population	371.9	360.7	401.8	410.4	403.0	407.3	432.5
Regional Share	13.2	12.1	11.7	11.6	11.4	11.2	11.0
STATE							
Population	2818.3	2978.2	3443.4	3537.1	3525.7	3626.1	3917.2
Regional Share	100.0	100.0	100.0	100.0	100.0	100.0	100.0

Source: *Census of Population, 1961-2002*

Table A4 Prices of Inner-city Residential Developments Launched 1995-March 1996, Expressed as Multipliers of Average Earnings (1995)

New prices 1995-6	Location	Launch Date	Av. Industrial Earnings			Av. Earnings Bank & Ins.		
			1 bed	2 bed	3 bed	1 bed	2 bed	3 bed
Bachelor's Walk	Dublin 1	May.95	2.43	4.68	5.49	1.93	3.72	4.36
Gt George's St Nth,	Dublin 1	Apr.95	2.78	4.71		2.22	3.76	
Northumberlands, Mount St. Lwr.	Dublin 2	Feb.95		4.49	5.06		3.57	4.02
The Cobbles, Essex St. E.	Dublin 2	Mar.95	3.31	3.93		2.63	3.12	
College Close, Tara St.	Dublin 2	Feb.95	3.18	3.74		2.53	2.97	
Dame St	Dublin 2	June.95	4.49			3.59		
The Granary, Temple Bar	Dublin 2	Feb.95	5.49		11.55	4.36		9.17
The Malt House, Grand Canal Q.	Dublin 2	June.95		5.87			4.68	
Mellor Court, Liffey St. Lwr.	Dublin 2	June.95	2.73	3.90		2.18	3.11	
The Cutlers, Exchange St.	Dublin 2	July.95	3.87	4.68	7.80	3.08	3.73	6.22
Green Building, Temple Bar	Dublin 2	Oct.95		4.68	7.49		3.81	6.10
Temple Bar Sq.	Dublin 2	Nov.95	4.68	5.18		3.70	4.10	
Trinity Court II, Lombard St.	Dublin 2	Mar.95	2.49	3.24	3.93	1.98	2.58	3.12
Portside Court, E.Wall Rd.	Dublin 3	Oct.95	2.81	3.24	3.62	2.29	2.64	2.95
The Waterside, Ringsend	Dublin 4	Apr.95	2.56	3.93		2.04	3.13	
Palatine Sq	Dublin 7	Oct.95		3.37			2.74	
Sarsfield House	Dublin 7	Mar.95	2.72	4.68		2.16	3.72	
Shandon Green, Phibsboro	Dublin 7	May.95		4.30			3.43	
Temple Court, U. Dominick St.	Dublin 7	Feb.95	1.93			1.53		

Table A4 Prices of Inner-city Residential Developments Launched 1995-March 1996, Expressed as Multipliers of Average Earnings (1995) – *continued*

Leonard's Court, Clanbrassil St.	Dublin 8	Feb.95		3.12			2.48	
Newmarket Sq.	Dublin 8	Sept.95	2.65	3.42	5.31	2.16	2.78	4.32
Hybreasal House, Kilmainham	Dublin 8	Sept.95	2.81	3.62		2.29	2.95	
The Maltings, Watling St.	Dublin 8	Nov.95	1.87	2.87		1.48	2.27	
Old Kilmainham Village, Bow La.	Dublin 8	Sept.95	2.68	3.49		2.18	2.84	
Portobello Dock	Dublin 8	Feb.95	3.68	4.93		2.92	3.91	
Portobello Dock	Dublin 8	Nov.95	3.55			2.81		
Usher's Quay	Dublin 8	Feb.95	2.37			1.88		
Mountjoy Sq.	Dublin 1	Feb.96	2.63	3.35		2.13	2.71	
Mountjoy Sq.	Dublin 1	Feb.96	2.33	3.35	5.08	1.88	2.71	4.11
Parnell St.	Dublin 1	Mar.96	2.33	3.53		1.88	2.85	
Stock Exchange Court, Cope St.	Dublin 2	Mar.96	5.08			4.11		
Charlotte Quay	Dublin 4	Jan.96	2.96	4.55		2.39	3.67	
Smithfield Village	Dublin 7	Mar.96	2.99	3.89	4.79	2.42	3.14	3.87
Leonard's Court, Clanbrassil St.	Dublin 8	Jan.96	2.51	3.29		2.03	2.66	

Source: Kelly and MacLaran (2004)

Table A5 Prices of Inner-city Residential Developments Launched November 2003, Expressed as Multipliers of Average Earnings

New prices Nov. 2003	Location	Av. Industrial Earnings			Av. Earnings Bank & Ins.		
		1 bed	2 bed	3 bed	1 bed	2 bed	3 bed
Spencer Dock	Dublin 1	10.78	12.13		8.69	9.78	
Portland Lock, Portland Pl.	Dublin 1	7.58	9.98		6.11	8.04	
Liberty Corner, James Joyce St.	Dublin 1		12.47	16.85		10.05	13.58
Bridgewater Hall, Summerhill Pd.	Dublin 1		11.96			9.65	
Gloucester Sq.	Dublin 1	9.61	12.30		7.74	9.92	
Quartier Bloom, Ormond Quay	Dublin 2		18.37			14.81	
Gallery Quay, Gd Canal Dock	Dublin 2	9.61	14.16	15.33	7.74	11.41	12.36
Adelaide Sq., Whitefriar St	Dublin 2		14.83			11.95	
Gasworks, Barrow St.	Dublin 4	10.45	13.48	18.87	8.42	10.87	15.21
Dock Mill, Barrow St.	Dublin 4	9.77	11.96	16.35	7.88	9.65	13.18
Smithfield Market	Dublin 7	12.13	14.49	17.69	9.78	11.68	14.26
Cork St, McGovern's Corner	Dublin 8		12.47	14.16		10.05	11.41
Grainstore, Marrowbone La.	Dublin 8		9.44			7.61	
Portobello Wharf, Harold's Cross Bridge	Dublin 8			24.43			19.70

Source: Kelly and MacLaran (2004)

References

Aalen, F. H. A. (1990) *The Iveagh Trust: The First Hundred Years* (Dublin, Iveagh Trust)

Aalen, F. H. A. (1992) "Health and Housing in Dublin c. 1850-1921", in: Aalen, F. H. A. and Whelan, K. (eds.) *Dublin City and County: From Prehistory to Present* (Dublin, Geography Publications).

All Party Oireachtas Committee on the Constitution (2004) *Ninth Progress Report: Private Property* (Dublin, Stationery Office)

Arnott, P. (1995) "Time for Revisionism on Rent Control?" *The Journal of Economic Perspectives* 9 (1), pp. 99-120.

Bacon, P. and Associates (1998) *An Economic Assessment of Recent House Price Developments* (Dublin, Report to the Minister for Housing and Urban Renewal).

Bacon, P. and Associates (1999) *The Housing Market: An Economic Review and Assessment* (Dublin, Report to the Minister for Housing and Urban Renewal).

Bacon, P. and Associates (2000) *The Housing Market in Ireland: An Economic Evaluation of Trends and Prospects,* (Dublin, Report to the Minister for Housing and Urban Renewal).

Bannon, Michael (1981) *Urbanisation: Problems of Growth* and Decay in Dublin, NESC Report 55 (Dublin, NESC)

Bannon, M. (2004a) "National Urban Policy is Badly Needed", *Irish Times*, 24 November 2004

Bannon, M. (2004b) "Forty Years of Irish Urban Planning: An Overview", *Journal of Irish Urban Studies*, 3 (1), pp. 1-16.

Bannon, M. (2004c) "Irish Urbanisation: Trends, Actions and

Policy Challenges", *Planning and Environmental Policy Research Series* (Dublin, Department of Planning and Environmental Policy, University College Dublin)

Bannon, M. (2005) "Planning for People: Observations on NESC chapter 5, Sustainable Neighbourhoods and Integrated Development", *Working Notes, 50*, Centre for Faith and Justice pp. 9-14.

Barlow, J., and Duncan, S. (1994) *Success and Failure in Housing Provision: European Systems Compared* (Oxford, Pergamon Press).

Barron, S. and Mulvany, F. (2005) *National Intellectual Disability Database* (Dublin, Health Research Board)

Bergin, E., Lalor, T., Lawless, K. and Pym, M. (2005) *Settlement First: Assessment of the Effectiveness of the Housing Act 1988 and Integrated Strategy 2000 in Meeting the Needs of People Who Are Homeless* (Dublin, The Simon Communities of Ireland)

BIPE (2000) *European Public Policy concerning Access to Housing*, Report to the European Commission (Boulogne Billancourt, France).

Blackwell, J. (1988) *A Review of Housing Policy* (Dublin, NESC Report No. 87)

Brady, P. (2000) "Still Waiting in Hope" in Sheehan, E. (ed.), *Travellers: Citizens of Ireland* (Dublin, Parish of the Travelling People)

Brooke, S. (2001), *Social Housing for the Future: Can Housing Associations Meet the Challenge?* (Dublin, Policy Institute Trinity College and Combat Poverty Agency).

Brooke, S. (2004) *Housing Problems and Irish Children: The Impact of Housing on Children's Wellbeing* (Dublin, Children's Research Centre, Trinity College Dublin)

Buchanan, C. (1969) *Regional Studies in Ireland* (Dublin, An Foras Forbartha).

Burns, M. (2005) "Housing the New Ireland: Comment on the NESC report". *Working Notes, 50*, Centre for Faith and Justice, pp. 2-8.

Callan, T. (1991) *Property Tax: Principles and Policy Options* (Dublin, Policy Research Paper No. 12, ESRI).

Casey, J. (2003) "An Analysis of Economic and Marketing Influences on the Construction Industry", *Building Industry Bulletin*, Dublin

CECODHAS (2005) *Social Housing in the European Union*, Report to the European Commission (Brussels, European Housing Observatory).

Central Bank and Financial Services Authority of Ireland (2004) "The Irish Housing Market: Fundamental and Non-Fundamental Influences", *Financial Stability Report*, pp. 51-73

Central Bank and Financial Services Authority of Ireland (2005) *Financial Stability Report*, pp. 5-33

Central Statistics Office (2004) *Census of Population, Volume 8 Irish Traveller Community* (Dublin, Stationery Office).

Combat Poverty Agency (1999) *Submission to Cross-Department Team on Homelessness, Department of the Environment* (Dublin, CPA)

Commission on Itinerancy (1963) *Report* (Dublin, Government of Ireland)

Commission on Taxation (1985) *Fourth Report: Special Taxation*, (Dublin, Stationery Office)

Commission on the Status of People with Disabilities (1995) *Report of the Working Group on Housing Accommodation* (Dublin)

Commission on the Status of People with Disabilities (1996) *Report: A Strategy for Equality* (Dublin)

Commission on the Private Rented Residential Sector (2000) *Report of the Commission on the Private Rented Residential Sector* (Dublin, Stationery Office).

Comptroller and Auditor General (2004) *The Grouped Schools Pilot Partnership Project* (Dublin, Government of Ireland)

Connolly, J. (1998) *Re-Righting the Constitution: The Case for New Social and Economic Rights* (Dublin: Irish Commission for Justice and Peace)

Connolly, J., (2002) Social and Economic Rights : A Rising Tide' in Punch M. and Buchanan, L (Eds), *Housing rights: A New Agenda* (Dublin, Threshold and Centre for Urban and Regional Studies)

Connolly, J. (2004) "Property Rights and the Right to Shelter", Submission to the All Party Committee on the Constitution: Private Property, pp.A27-29 (Dublin, Stationery Office).

Constitution Review Group (1996) *Report* (Dublin, Stationery Office)

CORI (2004) "Submission to the All-Party Oireachtas Committee on the Constitution", in All Party Oireachtas Committee on the Constitution *Ninth Progress Report: Private Property* (Dublin, Stationery Office)

CORI (2005) *Policy Briefing: Housing and Accommodation* (Dublin, CORI Justice Commission)

Coughlan, P. (1998) *Property Law* (Dublin, Gill and MacMillan)

CPSU and SIPTU (1998) *Affordable Accommodation: A Trade Union Issue and Human Right* (Dublin, CPSU and SIPTU)

DAFT (2005) *The Daft.ie Report* (Dublin, www.daft.ie)

Davidson, A. (1999) "Alternative Models of Social Housing: Tenure Patterns and Cost Renting in New Zealand and Sweden", *Housing Studies* 14 (4) pp. 453-472

Department of the Environment, Heritage and Local Government (2000) *Annual Housing Statistics Bulletin* (Dublin, Stationery Office)

Department of the Environment, Heritage and Local Government (2003) *Annual Housing Statistics Bulletin* (Dublin, Stationery Office)

Department of the Environment, Heritage and Local Government (2004) *Annual Housing Statistics Bulletin* (Dublin, Stationery Office)

Department of the Environment, Heritage and Local Government (2005) *Annual Housing Statistics Bulletin* (Dublin, Stationery Office)

Department of Social and Family Affairs (2005) *Statistical Report on Social Welfare Services* (Dublin, Stationery Office)

Dillon, B. (2004) *Changing Partners. How Public-Private Partnership has Replaced Community Partnership in Urban Regeneration: Causes and Consequences for St. Michael's Estate, Inchicore, Dublin* (Dublin, Nexus)

Downey, D. (1998) *New Realities in Irish Housing* (Dublin, CRUBE, Dublin Institute of Technology)

Downey, D. (2003) "Affordability and Access to Irish Housing: Trends, Policy and Prospects", *Journal of Irish Urban Studies*, 2 (1), pp. 1-24

Drudy, P. J. and MacLaran, A. (eds.) (2004) *Dublin: Economic and Social Trends,* Vol. 4, (Dublin, Centre for Urban and Regional Studies).

Drudy, P. J. et al. (1999) *Housing: A New Approach* (Dublin, Report of the Housing Commission, Irish Labour Party)

Drudy, P. J. and Punch, M. (2001) "Housing and Inequality in Ireland", in Cantillon, S., Corrigan, C., Kirby, P. and O'Flynn, J. (eds.) *Rich and Poor: Perspectives on Inequality in Ireland* (Dublin, Combat Poverty Agency and Oak Tree Press)

Drudy, P. J. and Punch, M (2002) "Housing Models and Inequality: Perspectives on Recent Irish Experience", *Housing Studies*, 17 (4), pp. 657-672

Dublin City Council (2002) *Regeneration/Next Generation* (Dublin, Dublin City Council).

Dublin City Council (2004) *St. Michaels Estate Framework Plan* (Dublin, Dublin City Council).

Dublin Docklands Development Authority (1997) *Dublin Docklands Area Master Plan* (Dublin, DDDA)

Dublin Local Authorities (1999) *Housing in Dublin: A Strategic Review by the Dublin Local Authorities* (Dublin, Dublin Corporation)

Duffy, David (2005) "The Performance of the Irish Housing

Market", Paper to a Statistical and Social Inquiry Society of Ireland Symposium, April, Dublin.

Economic Commission for Europe (1998) *Implementation of Human Settlement Policies on Urban Renewal and Housing Modernisation, Vienna Case Study* (New York, United Nations)

Economist, 18 June 2005

Edgar, B., Doherty, J. and Mina-Coull, A. (1999) *Services for Homeless People: Innovation and Change in the European Union* (Bristol, The Policy Press)

Edgar, B., Doherty, J. and Mina-Coull, A. (2000) *Support and Housing in Europe: Tackling Social Exclusion in the European Union* (Bristol, The Policy Press)

ESRI (1986) *Conditions of Traveller Accommodation*, (Dublin, ESRI Report 131)

European Central Bank (2003) *Structural Factors in EU Housing Markets* (Brussels, ECB)

European Commission (1999) *European Spatial Development Perspective* (Luxembourg, European Commission)

European Ministers (2002) *Final Communique of the Third European Ministers Conference on Sustainable Housing* (Genval, Belgium)

Evans, A. (2004) *Economics. Real Estate and the Supply of Land* (Oxford, Blackwell)

Fagan, R. (2004) "St. Michael's Estate – Our Story", Paper to the Combat Poverty Agency Seminar: *Putting Poverty and Social Exclusion at the Heart of Local Government* (Dublin, CPA).

Fahey, T. (ed.) (1999) *Social Housing in Ireland: A Study of Success, Failure and Lessons Learned*, (Dublin, Oak Tree Press)

Fahey, T. and Watson, D. (1995) *An Analysis of Social Housing Need* (Dublin, Economic and Social Research Institute)

Fahey, T., Nolan, B., Maitre, B. (2004) *Housing, Poverty and Wealth in Ireland* (Dublin, Institute of Pubic Administration and Combat Poverty Agency)

Fatima Groups Untied (2000) *Eleven Acres, Ten Steps* (Dublin, FGU)

Fatima Groups United (2004a) Presentation to the Threshold Seminar *The Regeneration Game: Urban Regeneration and Community Involvement* (Dublin, Threshold)

Fatima Groups United (2004b) *The Value of a Promise, the Promise of Value* (Dublin, FGU)

Finnerty J., (2002) "Homes for the Working Class? : Irish Public House-building Cycles, 1945-2001", *Saothar: Journal of Irish Labour History*, 27, pp. 65-71

Fitzgerald, E. and Winston, N. (forthcoming in 2005) "Housing, Equality and Inequality", in Norris, M. and Redmond, D. (eds.) *Housing in Contemporary Ireland: Economy, Society, Space and Shelter* (Dublin, Institute of Public Administration)

Fitzgerald, J. (2005) "The Irish Housing Stock: Growth in Number of Vacant Dwellings", *Quarterly Economic Commentary* Spring (Dublin, ESRI)

Fitzpatrick, T. and McQuinn, K. (2004) "House Prices and Mortgage Credit: Empirical Evidence for Ireland" (Dublin, Central Bank of Ireland Research Technical Paper, 5/RT/04)

Flood, Mr Justice Fergus M. (Chairman) (2002a), *Second Interim Report of the Tribunal of Inquiry into Certain Planning Matters and Payments* (Dublin, Stationery Office)

Flood, Mr Justice Fergus M. (Chairman) (2002b), *Third Interim Report of the Tribunal of Inquiry into Certain Planning Matters and Payments* (Dublin, Stationery Office)

Focus Ireland (2005) *Definition of Homelessness.* (http://www.focusireland.ie/htm/housing_homelessness/facts_figures/index.htm, Focus Ireland, last accessed June 2005)

Forrest, R., and Murie, A. (eds.) (1995) *Housing and Family Wealth: Comparative International Perspectives* (London, Routledge)

Forster, W. (1996) "Austria", in Balchin, P. (ed.) *Housing Policy in Europe* (London, Routledge)

Fraser, M. (1996) *John Bull's Other Homes: State Housing and British Policy in Ireland, 1883-1922* (Liverpool, Liverpool University Press)

Galligan, Y. (1999) "Housing policy in Ireland: continuity and change in the 1990's", in Collins, N. (ed.) *Issues in Irish Politics* (Manchester, Manchester University Press)

Government of Ireland (1991) *A Plan for Social Housing* (Dublin, Stationery Office)

Government of Ireland (1995) *Report of the Task Force on the Travelling Community* (Dublin, Stationery Office).

Government of Ireland (1999a) *Action on House Prices* (Dublin, Government Information Office)

Government of Ireland (1999b) *Towards Equal Citizenship: Progress Report on the Implementation of the Recommendations of the Commission on the Status of People with Disabilities* (Dublin, Stationery Office).

Government of Ireland (2000a) *Planning and Development Act, 2000,* (Dublin, Stationery Office)

Government of Ireland (2000b) *Homelessness: An Integrated Strategy* (Dublin, Stationery Office)

Government of Ireland (2002) *National Spatial Strategy.* (Dublin, Stationery Office)

Guerin, D. (1999) *Housing Income Support in the Private Rented Sector: A Survey of Recipients of SWA Rent Supplement* (Dublin, Combat Poverty Agency)

Gunne (2004) *The Residential Property Market 2003: An Analysis of the Facts* (Dublin, Gunne)

Hancock, K.E. (1993) "Can Pay? Won't Pay? Or Economic Principles of 'Affordability'", *Urban Studies,* 30 (1), pp.127-145

Hayden, A. (2004) *Irish Times,* 16 July 2004

Healy, J. (2004) *Housing, Fuel Poverty and Health: A Pan-European Analysis* (Aldershot, Ashgate Press)

International Monetary Fund (2000) "Ireland's property

Boom from an International Perspective", Selected Issues paper, (Washington, D.C., IMF)

International Monetary Fund (2003) *Ireland: Staff Report for the 2003 Article IV Consultation,* Dublin, May 2003 (Washington, D.C., IMF)

Joyce, D. (2000) "A New Response or the Same old Story ?" in Sheehan, Erica (ed.), *Travellers: Citizens of Ireland* (Dublin, Parish of the Travelling People)

Kearns, A. (2003), "Mortgage Arrears in the 1990s: Lessons for Today", *Central Bank Quarterly Bulletin, Autumn,* pp. 97-113, (Dublin, Central Bank and Financial Services Authority of Ireland).

Kelleher, P. and Whelan, M. (1992) *Dublin Communities in Action: A Study of Six Projects* (Dublin, Combat Poverty Agency)

Kelly, S. and MacLaran, A. (2004) The Residential Transformation of Inner Dublin, in: Drudy, P. J. and MacLaran, A. (Eds) *Dublin: Economic and Social Trends, Volume 4* (Dublin, Centre for Urban and Regional Studies).

Kelly, S. and Punch, M. (2005) "The regeneration of O'Devaney Gardens". Paper to the Centre for Urban and Regional Studies and Combat Poverty Agency Research Seminar *Community Participation in Urban Regeneration and Planning: Sharing the learning* (Dublin, Centre for Urban and Regional Studies).

Kemeny, J. (1995) *From Public Housing to the Social Market: Rental Policy Strategies in Comparative Perspective* (London, Routledge)

Kenna, P. (2001) The Role of Housing Strategies for Special Needs Housing. Paper to the Irish Council for Social Housing Biennial National Social Housing Conference (Westport, ICSH)

Kenna, P. (2002) "A Right to Housing: Is It More than a Mere Right to Shelter in Market Societies like Ireland?" in: Punch, M. and Buchanan, L. (eds) *Housing Rights: A New*

Agenda? (Dublin, Threshold and the Centre for Urban and Regional Studies)

Kenna, P. (2005) "The Impact of the European Convention on Human Rights on Social Housing Policy and Practice in Ireland", Paper to the Irish Council for Social Housing *Biennial National Social Housing Conference* (Sligo, ICSH)

Kenny, J. (1973) *Report of the Committee on the Price of Building Land* (Dublin, Stationery Office)

Kenny, G. (1998) "The Housing Market and the Macroeconomy: Evidence From Ireland" (Dublin, Central Bank of Ireland Research Technical Paper, 1/RT)

Kenny, B. (2004) "What Role Should Local Authorities Play in Social Housing Provision?" Paper to the Annual Housing Practitioners' Conference (Westport)

Korten, D. (1998) "Life after Capitalism" (http://www.pcdf.org/documents.htm, People Centered Development Forum, last accessed October 2005)

KPMG (1996) *Study of Urban Renewal Schemes,* (Dublin, Stationery Office)

Kuhn, T. (1957) *The Copernican Revolution: Planetary Astronomy in the Development of Western Thought* (Cambridge, Harvard University Press)

Kuhn, T. (1962) *The Structure of Scientific Revolutions* (Chicago, Chicago University Press)

Lawless, M. and Cox G. (2000) *From Residential Drug Treatment to Employment* (Dublin, Merchants Quay Project)

Lawless, M. and Corr, C. (2005) *Drug Use Among the Homeless Population in Ireland* (Dublin, National Advisory Committee on Drugs)

Lee, P., Murie, A. and Marsh, A. (1995) *The Price of Social Exclusion,* (London, National Federation of Housing Associations)

Lee, P., and Murie, A (1997) *Poverty, Housing Tenure and Social Exclusion,* (Bristol, The Policy Press)

MacLaran, A. (1993) *Dublin: the Shaping of a Capital* (London, Belhaven Press)

MacLaran, A. et al, (1995) *Recent Residential Development in Central Dublin,* (Dublin, Centre for Urban and Regional Studies, Trinity College).

McCashin, A. and Brooke, S. (2005) "Back to Blackwell", *Cornerstone: Magazine of the Homeless Agency,* April, pp. 8-10

McCashin, A. (2000) *The Private Rented Sector in the 21st Century: Policy Choices,* (Dublin, Threshold & St. Pancras Housing Association)

McGuirk P and MacLaran A (2001) "Changing Approaches to Urban Planning in an 'Entrepreneurial City': The Case of Dublin", *European Planning Studies* 9 (4), pp. 437-457

McManus, R. (2002) *Dublin, 1910-1940 : Shaping the City and Suburbs* (Dublin, Four Courts Press)

McNulty, P. (2003) "The Emergence of the Housing Affordability Gap", *Journal of Irish Urban Studies,* 2 (1) pp. 83-90

McQuinn, K (2004) "A model of the Irish housing sector" (Dublin, Central Bank of Ireland Research Technical Paper, 1/RT/04)

Mc Verry, P (1999) "Twenty-five Years of Homelessness", *Working Notes, 35*

Mc Verry, P. (2003) *The Meaning is in the Shadows* (Dublin, Veritas)

Ministerial Task Force (1996) *First Report of the Ministerial Task Force on Measures to Reduce the Demand for Drugs* (Dublin, Stationery Office)

Ministerial Task Force (1997) *Second Report of the Ministerial Task Force on Measures to Reduce the Demand for Drugs* (Dublin, Stationery Office)

Muir, J. (2004) "Public Participation in Area-Based Urban Regeneration Programmes", *Housing Studies,* 19 (6), pp. 947-966

Muir, J. (2005) "Regeneration and Participation: the Example of Ballymun", Paper to the Centre for Urban and Regional Studies and Combat Poverty Agency Research Seminar *Community Participation in Urban Regeneration and Planning: Sharing the Learning* (Dublin, CURS).

Mullins, D., Rhodes, M. L., and Williamson, A. (2003) *Non-Profit Housing Organisations in Ireland, North & South: Changing Forms and Challenging Futures* (Belfast, Northern Ireland Housing Executive)

Murray, K. and Norris, M. (2002) *Profile of Households Accommodated by Dublin City Council : Analysis of Socio-Demographic, Income and Spatial Patterns* (Dublin, Dublin City Council and Housing Unit)

National Economic and Social Council (1976) *Report on Housing Subsidies* (Dublin, NESC Report No. 23)

National Economic and Social Council (2004) *Housing in Ireland: Performance and Policy* (Dublin, NESC, No. 112)

National Economic and Social Forum (2000) *Social and Affordable Housing and Accommodation*, (Dublin, NESF)

National Traveller Accommodation Consultative Committee (2004) *Review of the Operation of the Traveller Accommodation Act 1998,* (Dublin, Report to the Minister for Housing and Urban Renewal)

Needham, B and De Kam, G (2000) *Land for Social Housing* (Brussels, European Liaison Committee on Social Housing)

Norris, M. and Shiels, P. (2004) *Regular National Report on Housing Developments in European Countries: Synthesis Report* (Dublin, Department of the Environment, Heritage and Local Government)

North Wall Community Association (1990) *North Wall News* (Dublin, NWCA)

North Wall Community Association (1993) *North Wall News* (Dublin, NWCA)

O'Brien, L. M. and Dillon, B. (1982) *Private Rented - The Forgotten Sector* (Dublin, Threshold)

O'Connell, T., and Quinn, T. (1999) "Recent Property Price

Developments: An Assessment", *Central Bank of Ireland, Bulletin,* (Dublin, Central Bank of Ireland)

O'Sullivan, E. (1996) *Homelessness and Social Policy in the Republic of Ireland* (Dublin, Department of Social Studies, Trinity College)

O'Sullivan, E. (1999) *National Report on Housing in Ireland,* (Brussels, FEANTSA)

O'Sullivan, E. (2004) "Welfare Regimes, Housing and Homelessness in the Republic of Ireland", *European Journal of Housing Policy,* 4 (3), pp. 323-343.

O'Sullivan, L. (2002) *Accommodation Disadvantage: A Study to Identify Women's Accommodation Experiences, Useful Data Sources and Major Research Gaps* (Dublin, Threshold)

O'Sullivan, L. (2005), *The Determinants of House Prices in Ireland* (Dublin, Mimeo, Department of Economics, Trinity College, Dublin)

O'Sullivan, T. and Gibb, K. (eds.) (2003) *Housing Economics and Public Policy* (Oxford, Blackwell Science Ltd)

O'Toole, F. (2003) *After the Ball* (Dublin, TASC at New Island)

Paris, Chris (ed.) (2001) *Housing in Northern Ireland and Comparisons with the Republic of Ireland* (Coventry, Chartered Institute of Housing)

Parkin, M. et al. (2003) *Economics* (London, Pearson Addison Wesley)

Power, A. (1993) *Hovels to High Rise: State Housing in Europe Since 1850* (London, Routledge)

Power, A. (2004) *Sustainable Communities and Sustainable Development: A Review of the Sustainable Communities Plan* (London, UK Sustainable Development Commission)

Punch, M., Hickey, C., Buchanan, L, and Bergin, E. (2002), *Housing Access for All? An Analysis of Housing Strategies and Homeless Action Plans* (Dublin, Focus Ireland, Simon Communities of Ireland, St. Vincent de Paul, Threshold)

Punch, M. and Drudy, P.J. (2002) "Housing Models and Housing Rights: A Framework for Discussion" in Punch

M. and Buchanan, L (eds,), *Housing Rights: A New Agenda*, pp. 87-95 (Dublin, Threshold and Centre for Urban and Regional Studies)

Punch, M. (forthcoming in 2005) "Uneven Development and the Private Rental Market: Problems and Prospects for Low-Income Households", in: Norris, M. and Redmond, D. (eds.) *Housing Contemporary Ireland: Economy, Society, Space and Shelter* (Dublin, Institute of Public Administration)

Redmond, D. (2001) "Social Housing in Ireland: Under New Management?", *European Journal of Housing Policy*, 1 (2) pp. 291-306

Redmond, D. and Kernan, G. (2004) "Housing Policy, Home Ownership and the Provision of Affordable Housing", in Scott, M. and Moore, N. (eds) *Renewing Urban Communities: Environment, Citizenship and Sustainability in Ireland* (Aldershot, Ashgate Press)

Roche, M. (2003) "Will there be a crash in Irish house prices?" *ESRI Quarterly Economic Commentary*, Winter, pp 57-72

Roche, D. (2005) Quoted in *Irish Times*, 2 June 2005

St. Michael's Estate Regeneration Team (2002) *Past, Present, Future: A Community Vision for the Regeneration of St. Michael's Estate* (Dublin: St. Michael's Estate Blocks Committee)

Simon Communities of Ireland (1995) *The Homeless* (http://www.simoncommunity.com/pages/aboutus/the-homeless.htm, Simon Communities of Ireland, last accessed June 2005)

Smith N. (1996) *The New Urban Frontier: Gentrification and the Revanchist City* (London, Routledge)

Sweeney, P. (2004) *Selling Out? Privatisation in Ireland*, (Dublin, TASC at NEW Island)

Tax Strategy Group (2004) *Tax Incentives/Expenditures and Broadening of the Tax Base*, TSG 04/22/ (Dublin, Department of Finance)

Threshold (2002) *Strategic Plan* (Dublin, Threshold)

Threshold (2005) *Seeking a Home on Rent Supplement: Experience in Cork City in 2004* (Cork, Threshold)

Todaro, M. and Smith, S. (2005), *Economic Development* (Harlow, Pearson, Addison, Wesley)

Turner, B. (1996) "Sweden", in Balchin, P. (ed.) *Housing Policy in Europe,* (London, Routledge)

United Nations Committee on Economic, Social and Cultural Rights (2002) *Second Periodic Report* (Geneva, United Nations)

United Nations Economic and Social Council (2002) *Concluding Observations of the Committee on Economic, Social and Cultural Rights: Ireland,* 5 June 2002 (Geneva, United Nations)

United Nations Office of the High Commissioner for Human Rights (1991) *The Right to Adequate Housing,* General Comment No. 4 (Geneva, United Nations)

Whyte, G. (2002) *Social Inclusion and the Legal System: Public Interest Law in Ireland* (Dublin, Institute of Public Administration)

Williams, R. (1989) *Resources of Hope* (London, Verso)

Yamada, Y. (1999) "Affordability crises in Housing in Britain and Japan", *Housing Studies* 14 (1), pp. 99-110

Index

October 2005

The Report of the Democracy Commission

Engaging Citizens
The Case for Democratic Renewal in Ireland

Edited by Clodagh Harris

David Begg,
Ivana Bacik, Ruth Barrington, John Hanafin, Bernadette MacMahon,
Elizabeth Meehan, Nora Owen, Donal Toolan, Tony Kennedy, Mark
Mortell, Caroline Wilson

'We think we have come as close as is possible to getting a clear picture of the health of democracy in both parts of Ireland. We hope that our conclusions will, in the course of time, strengthen democracy on the island of Ireland and support those who make it work.' David Begg.

Establishing the Commission was the initiative of two think tanks, TASC in Dublin and Democratic Dialogue in Belfast. Launched in 2003 the Commission was asked to enquire into the causes of disconnection for large groups of people from even the most basic forms of democratic participation in decision-making. The members of the independent commission, acting in a voluntary capacity, made public engagement the cornerstone of their work.

The report of the Commission has been described as a really excellent and thought provoking document on all the fronts it addresses. It draws on - and directs readers to - recent research in all areas, and yet is really accessible'

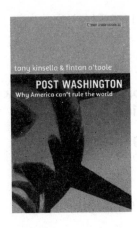

June 2005

Post Washington
Why America can't rule the world

by **Tony Kinsella and Fintan O'Toole**

Has the American Dream been replaced by the American myth?

The United States is the largest military, economic and cultural power in history. The aspirational focus of billions, the US leads the world into a brighter tomorrow, a tomorrow modelled exclusively on its own achievements. Our future lies in a US Imperium.

But, just as the sun sets on a *Pax Brittanica*, has it yet to even rise on a *Pax Americana?* Here writer and commentator Tony Kinsella and Irish Times' journalist and author Fintan O'Toole, argue that the United States of America is not only incapable of maintaining its dominant position in the world, but that this dominance is, at the very least, exaggerated and over-estimated.

Post Washington argues that the US system cannot continue. An extraordinary fragile economy straddles an agricultural sector on the verge of disaster, while the level of public and private debt threatens to topple a social and political structure crying out for reform.

At the dawn of the 21st century, the greatest threat to America comes from within. 'The world cannot wait for the US to wake from its slumber', say the authors. 'We must move on, building our post-Washington world- with the US where possible, but without it where necessary.'

May 2005

For Richer, For Poorer
A investigation into the Irish
Pension System

edited by Jim Stewart

With current pension policy widening income inequality in Irish
society, a large proportion of our pensioners, particularly women,
will be without adequate income in their old age.

For Richer, For Poorer sets out a radical and revised criteria for our pension system, outlining key proposals on what should constitute a
pension strategy for Ireland.

Provocative and timely, *For Richer, For Poorer* argues that our current
system is skewed towards the better off. Exposing a system that has
evolved to serve the interests of the pension industry, the book
offers both a critical evaluation of this system and makes clear policy recommendations.

With Peter Connell on demographics; Gerard Hughes on the cost of
tax expenditures; Tony McCashin on the State Social security system; Jim Stewart on sources of income to the retired population, Sue
Ward on the UK pension system, *For Richer, For Poorer* explores the
problems with the current system, and recommends that while the
UK has been our guide, it should not be our model.

November 2004

An Outburst of Frankness
Community arts in Ireland
– a Reader

edited by **Sandy Fitzgerald**

An Outburst of Frankness is the first serious attempt to gather together a wide range of views dealing with the history, theory and practice of community arts in Ireland. Not an academic book, the style, over twelve commissioned essays and the edited transcripts of two unique fora, is accessible and open, ranging from a general art-history perspective to the particular experiences of artists working in and with communities.

Besides the politics, the rhetoric and the debates, there are values around this activity called community arts which are as relevant today as they were forty or four hundred years ago. At the core of these values is the question of power and the right of people to contribute to and participate fully in culture; the right to have a voice and the right to give voice. From this point of view, arts and culture should be at the centre of all political, social, educational, individual and communal activity, particularly in this time of unprecedented and sometimes dangerous change, for Ireland and the world.

October 2004

Selling Out?
Privatisation in Ireland

by **Paul Sweeney**

This is the story of privatisation in Ireland – who made money, who lost money and whether the taxpayer gained. It sets the limits on privatisation – what should not be sold for money – and it shows that privatisation is about not only ownership but also public influence and control. It proves that this government has already sold out key assets, that consumers now pay higher prices and competitiveness has been lost. Examining the story of the Eircom privatisation, Sweeney shows how this triumph for 'popular capitalism' was, in fact, a hard lesson in why some state assets should never be privatised.

Sweeney quantifies the billions in gains made by the state on its investments in the state companies and how much the remaining companies are worth, and he proposes reforms to dynamise the remaining state companies to the advantage of the taxpayer, the consumer, society and the economy.

October 2003

After the Ball

by Fintan O'Toole

Is it the death of communal values? Or the triumph of profit? In a series of sharply observed essays, Fintan O'Toole the award-winning *Irish Times* commentator, looks at Ireland's growing notoriety as one of the most globalised yet unequal economies on earth. Why were the boom years haunted by the spectre of a failing health service? Why do a substantial proportion of our children continue to be marginalised through lack of funding in education? What is the place of people with disabilities, travellers, women immigrants and asylum-seekers in our brave new land?

Passionate and provocative, *After the Ball* is a wake-up call for a nation in transition. Irish people like to see Ireland as a exceptional place. In this starting polemic, Fintan O'Toole shatters the illusion once and for all.

Support TASC
A think tank for Action on Social Change

> 'the limited development of think tanks is a striking feature [of Ireland]
> for such bodies could do much to focus new thinking about the country's
> future democratic and political development'

(REPORT TO THE
JOSEPH ROWNTREE CHARITABLE TRUST, 2002)

Ireland almost uniquely in Europe has relatively few think tanks of
any kind and, prior to the establishment of TASC, none whose sole
agenda is to foster new thinking on ways to create a more progressive and equal society. Such an independent public policy think
tank is long overdue and urgently needed in Ireland.

Your support is essential - to do its work TASC must keep a distance from political and monetary pressure in order to protect the
independence of its agenda. If you would like to make a contribution to TASC – A Think Tank for Action on Social Change, please
send your donation to the address below

DONATIONS TO:
TASC
A Think Tank for Action on Social change
26 Sth Frederick St, Dublin 2.
Ph: 00353 1 6169050
Email:contact@tascnet.ie
www.tascnet.ie